LUNCHBOX TREATS

LUNCHBOX TREATS

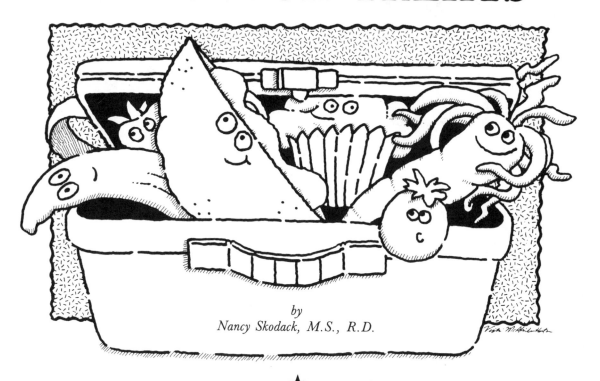

by
Nancy Skodack, M.S., R.D.

★

TexasMonthlyPress

Note: The information presented in this book is intended for most healthy school-age children with normal dietary needs. Always seek the advice of your family physician or pediatrician about any health matter, including specific nutritional requirements during illness.

Texas Monthly Press
P.O. Box 1569
Austin, Texas 78767

A   B   C   D   E   F   G   H

Library of Congress Cataloging-in-Publication Data

Skodack, Nancy, 1951-
  Lunch box treats / Nancy Skodack.
    p.   cm.
  ISBN 0-87719-110-7 : $8.95
  1. Lunchbox cookery.   I. Title.
TX735.S56   1989
641.5'3 — dc20   89-36352
Book design by Vicki McAlindon Horton   CIP

To Katy,
my first little treat

CONTENTS

ACKNOWLEDGMENTS

No book is ever written alone. Many people made this dream come true, and for their participation, I wish to thank them.

To the parents, principals, and teachers who responded to my nutrition surveys and enthusiastically endorsed the need for this book;

To the dedicated readers of my newspaper column who challenged me to compile my everyday health advice into a cookbook for parents and kids;

To my dear friends Dave and Lyn Johnson, who took time, energy, and resources away from their own business to help me research the market for this book;

To my pal Val Rowe, who nurtured the concept of this book through its infancy with her creative talent;

To Lee Gilmer, for his inspiring margin notes in the proofreading of my proposal;

To my whole family, especially my parents, for their extraordinary assistance in kid management;

To my quality-control subcommittee: Kathryn, Stephen, Kevin, and Sarah;

To the infinite wisdom, loving patience, and tireless tastebuds of my husband, Terry;

To my mother, Joette Davis, with appreciation for her contribution in managing our complicated family life;

To Scott Lubeck and the staff at Texas Monthly Press, who gave me an *A* for effort;

Thank you all.

INTRODUCTION

As parents, we worry about what kinds of foods our children are eating while away from home—with good reason.

Lunchtime meals should account for at least one third of the daily energy, fiber, vitamin, and mineral needs of a healthy kid. Yet often, school lunch menus are limited and dull. Worse, between-meal snacks are loaded with calories and offer little nutrition — a daily food formula that adds up to poor concentration in the classroom.

As members of the health-conscious majority, we are uneasy about the nutritional value of mass-produced meals and overpackaged convenience foods. And kids agree. Marketing research confirms that more than 13 million students pass up the cafeteria chow each year for mini-meals packed from home.

Remembering favorite lunchbox treats of the past, we search for ways to offer the same nurturing noontime experiences to our own children. But times have changed. Somewhere between aerobics, business clients, chauffeuring, after-school activities, and dinnertime, we have lost the blueprint on how to balance foods basic to a healthy lifestyle.

And so, *Lunchbox Treats* was created. Here, you will find the ABC's of children's chowtime and more. Four separate resources have been combined into a convenient package:

- *a refresher course* on how to create a varied and nutritious midday meal for children
- *a menu planner* to simplify the exasperating task of deciding what to fix fast
- *an everyday cookbook* with 120 practical recipes for healthy kid meals, and
- *a catalog* of innovative ideas to take the boredom out of school lunches.

Based on more than two years of consumer research, this cookbook is especially suited to the fast pace of American life and work. Most of the recipes in the collection have been reduced to ten steps or fewer. And since the directions are so easy to follow, why not let the kids join in the fun?

Another shortcut to savor: *Lunchbox Treats* is organized by season of the year, with attention to food availability, the school calendar, and of course holidays. This feature will enable you to prepare food for a school party, birthday celebration, or holiday event in the twinkling of an eye.

If packing lunchboxes is a chore usually performed long after the kids have gone to bed, you'll find whimsical menus that turn this nutritional nightmare into delightful daydreams. Move to the head of the class while serving Thesis on Tuna, Pita Principles, Fieldwork in Fruit, and Yogurt 101. Chuckle in the holiday humor of Ham-It-Up Salad, Waffle Wedges, Three-Fruit Toss, and Corny Chowder. Join the kids on center stage for the Asparaguys, Star-Studded Pasta, Broadway Blondies, and Symphony in Milk.

Speaking of kids, a child won't get any nourishment from a well-balanced meal if he throws it away. The recipes in *Lunchbox Treats* have been designed to appeal to the highly trained tastebuds of the school-age child. And because kids are equipped with special scanning devices to detect unidentified food objects, the recipes emphasize the familiar and favorite.

In designing the lunchbox menus, a panel of kid experts, along with their parents and teachers, presented the following challenges:

- For starters, all of the treats must really taste good.
- To take top honors, the delicious category must include nutritious foods basic to good health.
- For outstanding achievement, the recipes selected should conjure up some creativity in the kitchen.

- Finally, a first-class lunch from home, the brown-bag experts say, includes a special treat from Mom or Dad. So the book is complete with a few surprises for the small fry that help school spirits to soar.

  Kids are never shy about telling you exactly what they like. It pleases me to report that the cafeteria scholars, and the parents and faculty, participating in the taste test gave *Lunchbox Treats* a gold star. Have fun with this book. It is packed with healthy menu advice that I hope you will find useful long after your child graduates from lunchboxes to lunch briefs.

Nancy Skodack

A NOTE TO PARENTS

Cooking is a family affair. I encourage you to browse through the kitchen with your child. Include the range top, oven, refrigerator, dishwasher, and microwave oven on the tour. Pay special attention to the blender, food processor, hand mixer, electric can opener, and other time-saving appliances. Talk about how the equipment operates and who has permission to use it. The last stop should include a serious discussion on knives and other sharp utensils. Be sure to include a road map for safety, and give enough grown-up guidance to make sure those directions are followed — without detours.

BACK TO BASICS

*A nutrition glossary
for healthier
meals away from home*

Balanced diet: A sensible daily eating plan with the right nutrients, in the proper amounts, and with enough variety to promote health.

Basic food groups: A simple grouping of foods that serves as the foundation of a nutritionally sound eating plan. Each food is assigned to one of the following four groups according to its major nutrient contribution: meats; milk and milk products; breads, cereals, and whole grains; fruits and vegetables.

Carbohydrate: A major source of energy supplied to the body in the foods we eat.

Carbohydrates help your body to use the fuel from fat more effectively and spare protein for other important duties. That's why health experts recommend that 50 percent to 55 percent of daily calories come from this source. There are three different kinds of carbohydrates in the catalog of foods that we eat:

- *Complex carbohydrates* have the highest health score. They are warehouses of energy and sources of the vitamins, minerals, and protein essential to good health. Choose whole-grain breads and fortified cereals, vegetables, pasta, potatoes in their skins, nuts, brown rice, beans, and seeds to boost dietary fiber.

- *Simple carbohydrates* rate an *A* for energy. They occur naturally in fruits and some vegetables, and the body makes a short subject of their nutrient-rich quick-energy supply.

- *Refined carbohydrates* like table sugar, syrups, honey, and jellies provide calories for energy needs and little else.

Cholesterol: A fatty substance supplied by some foods and manufactured in the liver. Cholestrol lines up in the bloodstream to build cell membranes and make hormones. In general, foods derived from animals supply most of the cholesterol in our diets. Vegetables, fruits, and grains are of plant origin and contain no cholesterol. Diets rich in saturated fats have a tendency to raise blood cholesterol. Too much cholesterol circulating in the bloodstream has been shown to increase dramatically the risk for coronary heart disease.

Fat: A concentrated source of energy supplied to the body in foods we eat. Fat is also manufactured inside the body when we consume more carbohydrates and proteins than the body needs. It is assigned as the carrier for fat-soluble vitamins A, D, E, and K, among other duties. But too much of a good thing is not healthy. Most medical authorities agree that a healthy diet should consist of 30 percent or less fat. Some fat facts to remember:

- *Saturated fats,* frequently solid at room temperature, are found in animal products like meat fat, poultry skin, butter, shortening, and lard. They are also present in some tropical vegetable oils such as palm oil, palm kernel oil, and coconut oil. Saturated fats have a tendency to raise blood cholesterol levels.

- *Unsaturated fats* are most often liquid at room temperature. Research indicates that this type of fat tends to lower blood cholesterol. You'll find *polyunsaturated fat* abundantly in safflower, sunflower, corn, soybean, cottonseed, and partially hydrogenated cottonseed oil. Examples of *monosaturated fats* include olives, peanuts, and avocados.

Fiber: Fine tunes the intestinal tract to keep it in proper working order, thus aiding the process of digestion. Although fiber is not a nutrient, it is plentiful in many foods, including whole grains, nuts, fruits, and vegetables. Some studies suggest that it may even play a role in the prevention of certain types of cancer. Fiber excels in two categories:

- *Insoluble fiber* has been a stable performer on the nutritional scorecard in the forms of cellulose, hemicellulose, and lignin. These fast-track veterans have earned a reputation for moving food through the body's intestinal system with wheat bran and other whole grains.

- *Soluble fiber* forms a gel with water as it passes through the intestine. But that's only part of the story. Research shows this group of fat-finders may help reduce the risk of heart disease by lowering the levels of cholesterol circulating in the bloodstream. Pectin and gums are first-class fibers plentiful in oat bran, fruits, dried beans, and peas.

Minerals: Inorganic compounds that perform vital roles in the regulation of body functions. The double duty performed by minerals in the building and maintenance of bones and teeth is widely recognized. Their other claims to fame include involvement in the transportation of oxygen and the manufacture of important enzymes and hormones. Experts advise eating a balanced diet regularly to get a good share of minerals in the proportions needed for good health. These super-star substances can be thought of as belonging to one of two teams:

- *Macrominerals* are required in larger amounts, relatively speaking. This group of heavy hitters includes calcium, phosphorus, potassium, sulfur, sodium, magnesium, and chloride.

- *Microminerals* are no less important, but they are needed in much smaller amounts. Sometimes called trace elements, this lineup contains iron, manganese, copper, iodine, fluoride, zinc, molybdenum, selenium, and chromium.

Nutrients: Substances constantly needed by the body to maintain life. Nutrients include carbohydrates, fats, proteins, vitamins, minerals, and water. The first three — carbohydrates, fats, and proteins — are major energy contributors to the diet. Vitamins, minerals, and water are not energy sources, but they participate in the release of energy through body processes.

Nutrition: A group of related processes furnishing the body with the fuel needed to fulfill energy requirements, to support growth, and to repair and replace its parts.

Protein: A hardworking nutrient that builds, repairs, and maintains body tissues, as well as assisting with other body processes. Despite its importance, health professionals recommend that just 15 percent of daily calories come from this nutrient. Signing up for extra protein brings extracurricular fat and calories, too.

The building blocks of protein are called amino acids. The body can break down and rearrange amino acids from the diet into new tissues. Amino acids that cannot be reconstructed in that fashion must be supplied in the required form as a part of the protein we eat. For that reason, they are called essential amino acids.

- *Complete proteins* contain essential amino acids. They are widely found in animal sources, including beef, fish, poultry, eggs, and dairy products.

- *Incomplete proteins* lack one or more of the essential amino acids. Plants supply these proteins in the form of beans, peas, nuts, grains, and seeds. Complementary vegetable proteins can be teamed up to make a complete protein. Peanut butter on whole-wheat bread, for example, will provide complete protein, and so will rice served with beans.

Sodium: A mineral that occurs naturally in some foods and drinking water. Sodium is on the safety patrol inside the body, balancing fluids in the bloodstream, helping the heart and other muscles to contract, and assisting nerves in sending out signals. One third of the sodium in the diet is from table salt (sodium chloride). Much of the other two thirds comes from processed foods that contain sodium in the forms of disodium phosphate, monosodi-um glutamate, sodium bicarbonate, and sodium nitrate, to name a few. Too much sodium can cause problems for people who are sensitive to high blood pressure. Since most of us eat far more salt than our bodies need, many health practitioners think it's a good idea to shake the salt habit.

Variety: A curriculum that enables us to choose our foods according to individual needs. Each person has differing nutritional requirements based on factors like age, sex, body size, activity, and state of health. No single food provides all of the nutrients needed by the body, so it's best to boost your health score with the extra credit of variety.

Vitamins: Organic compounds needed in small amounts for the regulation of body processes. Vitamins are best known as energy busters, working to free the energy from carbohydrates, proteins, and fats to make it available for use in the body. They're also important to growth, vision, healthy bones and teeth, resistance to infection, and more. They are usually classified according to solubility.

- *Fat-soluble vitamins* dissolve in fats and oils. After we obtain them from the foods we eat, our bodies can conveniently store them. The fat-soluble vitamins include vitamins A, D, E, and K. (Could you guess that vitamin A was the first of the vitamins to be discovered?)
- *Water-soluble vitamins* dissolve in water. They are easily destroyed during the preparation of food and cannot be stored by the body, so they must be supplied to the body regularly. This group includes vitamin C and the B vitamins: thiamine, riboflavin, vitamin B-6, vitamin B-12, folacin, and niacin. Water-soluble vitamins are well represented in lean meats, fish, milk and milk products, whole grain and enriched cereals, citrus fruits and juices, and dark green, leafy vegetables.

Water: One of the essential nutrients needed to maintain life. Water accounts for about two thirds of the body's weight. It acts as a bus to transport other nutrients and remove body wastes. Water also aids digestion and helps to regulate body temperature. It is important to drink plenty of water to satisfy thirst. The body needs six to eight glasses of water each day.

SCHOOL LUNCHES THAT MAKE THE GRADE

*A helpful guide to
creating a daily eating plan that is
balanced, nutritious, and delicious*

For years the word "nutrition" didn't create much excitement for the general public. It was just something we studied in grade school—and promptly forgot. Happily, however, one of the by-products of the new American health movement has been a rekindled interest in nutrition and our old grade-school buddies, the basic four food groups.

The famous four (meats; milk and milk products; breads, cereals, and whole grains; fruits, and vegetables) have been given a face-lift in recent years by the Center for Science in the Public Interest. The food groups are now part of a new and more flexible framework designed to help us make healthier food choices. The long and short of it is this: a sensible eating plan includes a variety of foods, in the right proportion, in moderate amounts, and with careful attention to health value.

Variety is just one chapter in the recommended eating plan. No single food contains all of the nutrients needed for health, and some foods supply more nutrients than others. That's why it is best to vary daily food selections. Eating a wide variety of foods basic to good health helps to achieve nutritional balance, the second topic in the course outline.

Balance is essential for the body to operate efficiently. Most nutrients perform their best work when joined by other nutrients. The process is much like accounting. The gains from supplying nutrition-packed foods to the body are calculated daily against the losses from the repair and replacement of body parts and the burning of stored calories for energy. The nutritional books must balance if the body is to stay healthy. Too much is as undesirable as too little. So no refresher course is complete without including the principle of moderation.

Moderation means more than just restricting the undesirable foods in your daily diet. The only foods truly off-limits are those eaten in excess, so practice prudence. Portion control will make it easier to stay within the guidelines.

Let's review. For a health difference you can calculate, plug the principles of variety, balance, and moderation into your child's nutrition formula. Keeping those important basics in mind, it's time for a lesson on how to build a better lunchbox meal.

Eating: A Recommended Daily Pattern (National Dairy Council, Rosemont, Illinois, 1987), and *The Dietary Guidelines: Seven Ways to Help Yourself to Good Health and Nutrition* (American Dietetic Association, Chicago, 1987).

The following food lists are adapted from *Exchange Lists for Meal Planning* (American Diabetes Association and the American Dietetic Association, Alexandria, Virginia, 1986), *Guide to Good*

MEAT, FISH, POULTRY, AND OTHER PROTEIN SOURCES

Include these foods as good sources of protein to build and repair the body. They also contain valuable B vitamins and microminerals like iron and zinc. Each of the following portions equals a two-ounce serving moderate in fat that packs the power of protein:

½ cup boneless baked, boiled, or roasted
chicken or turkey
(without the skin)

2 slices of 97 percent lean boiled ham
(1 ounce each)

½ cup water-packed tuna

2 ounces cooked and trimmed lean beef
(such as ground round,
rump roast, or round steak)

½ cup diced, cooked lean pork loin

To add variety, try one of these protein sources. Each serving has about the same health score as one ounce of meat:

2 tablespoons of peanut butter

¼ cup cottage cheese
(Encourage low-fat varieties.)

½ cup cooked dried beans, peas, or lentils

¼ cup nuts such as pecans or walnuts

1 whole egg or 2 egg whites

MILK, CHEESE, AND YOGURT

Load up the lunchbox with the goodness of calcium, protein, and B vitamins from this family of foods. Each one of the servings below makes a nutrient contribution similar to an eight-ounce glass of milk.

1 cup yogurt
(Whenever possible, select
plain nonfat or low-fat varieties.)

1 ½ ounces cheese
(Part-skim mozzarella, farmer,
reduced-fat Swiss, or modified
cheddar-type cheeses provide
less fat.)

⅓ cup nonfat dry milk powder

1 cup homemade milk pudding

½ cup undiluted canned evaporated
skimmed milk

BREADS, CEREALS, AND WHOLE GRAINS

Give a B-vitamin boost with servings from the bread, cereal, and grain group. Iron and fiber come along for the ride with this pick. And when you choose whole grains and enriched or fortified cereal products, you are furnishing a rich supply of energy to the body in the form of carbohydrates. Charge up chowtime with these one-serving sources.

½ cup cooked pasta

1 six-inch whole-wheat or corn tortilla

1 homemade muffin or pancake or slice of whole-grain bread

½ cup cooked rice

½ pita pocket bread or ½ bagel

FRUIT

First-class fruits add vitamins, minerals, and fiber to the menu. Their variety is endless, with dried, fresh, frozen, unsweetened, or juice-packed fruits and unsweetened natural fruit juices. We look to these foods to supply vitamins A and C for a growing child. Oranges, grapefruits, melons, and strawberries are kid pleasers famous for their vitamin C contribution. For vitamin A, try apricots or cantaloupe. How about one of these treats for the lunch bag? (Each equals one serving.)

½ cup water-packed canned fruit or
1 cup frozen whole unsweetened strawberries

7 dried apricot halves

12 to 15 seedless grapes or
⅓ of a small cantaloupe or
1 whole medium piece of fruit

½ cup unsweetened natural fruit juice

VEGETABLES

Packing a variety of vegetables is the key to adding crunch and color to noontime nibbling. Most vegetables are high in fiber, low in calories, and a good source of vitamins A and C. Color is the best clue when searching for vegetables rich in vitamin A. Those that rate an *A* include dark green or deep yellow sources such as spinach, squash, sweet potatoes, and carrots. Cauliflower and broccoli are great choices for vitamin C. Try these one-serving suggestions:

½ cup unsalted vegetable juice or
½ cup cooked vegetables

1 cup raw vegetables
(Carrot and celery sticks, cauliflower pieces, broccoli florets, and asparagus spears are good starts.)

1 whole fresh tomato
(a fruit most often used as a vegetable)

1 tossed green salad

EXTRAS

It is true that as grown-ups, most of us eat too many servings from the extras list. Additions like salad dressing, honey, ketchup, oil, sugar, margarine, syrup, mustard, and pickle relish are concentrated sources of calories. But keep in mind that this collection of recipes is designed for growing kids with energy demands far greater than our own. Used in moderation, these extras can enhance flavors while providing children with an additional source of calories to grow on. After all, your efforts will have been for nothing if the nutritious lunch you packed comes right back home. In limited quantities, extras are okay and can help nutrient-dense foods pass the taste test of tiny tastebuds.

LUNCH PACKING TIPS

Practical pointers for lunchbox treats
that are fast to fix and stay safe to eat

Yes, there is an art to loading the lunchbox so that the tasty treats are just right when lunchtime arrives. Here are some suggestions you may find helpful in keeping those movable meals in their prime:

- An important rule of thumb: keep cold foods cold and hot foods hot. Perishable cold items should be packed only after being thoroughly chilled, and hot foods need to be prepared at the last minute and loaded while piping hot.
- Splurge on the latest lunchbox tools to keep foods safe to eat, like insulated containers, commercial cold packs, and thermos cups.

- A wise parent labels every item in the lunchbox to avoid confusion in the cafeteria. If you're packing something new or you think your child may forget what goes with what, send along directions. Freezer tape works great for this.
- For extra protection, wrap each muffin or cookie individually in plastic wrap before packing them in the lunchbox. It's best to wrap these treasures just after baking to preserve freshness. You'll save valuable loading time later in the week if the goodies are already wrapped and ready to go.
- To keep hot liquids like soup or cider nice and warm until lunch, preheat the thermos at the last possible moment before filling it. First, fill the thermos with boiling water. Wait a few minutes. Pour out the hot water. Fill the prepared thermos with the hot beverage. Seal it tight.

- If some parts of the feast are fragile, try this tip: Insulate the top and bottom of the lunch container with plastic bubble pack, crumpled newspaper (the comics are fun) or polystyrene packing material.
- Always wrap foods like lettuce, tomatoes, carrot sticks, or sliced pickles separately from the sandwich. Don't forget that salad dress-ups and tangy toppers belong in their own tiny containers. Be sure to secure the lids with tape.
- To help your kids lighten their load, use plastic or paper disposables when possible. For a change of pace, make lunch fun with special theme days. Festive plates with coordinated napkins and cups can make a birthday in the cafeteria an event to remember. Tuck in a party favor for a lunch friend.
- Pack foods and containers into the lunchbox or bag snugly so they won't move around. Load heavier objects at the bottom and lighter ones near the top. Need to keep those delicate cookies from crumbling? Wrap each cookie individually in plastic. Tape the cookies to the inside of the lunchbox lid with masking tape. It works!
- During warmer months, pack anything you can frozen. Bread, juice packs, muffins, and cookies do well in the freezer. Spread sandwich fillings between slices of frozen bread. Place chicken or turkey slices between halves of a frozen muffin. For less fat, hold the mayonnaise.
- Take a quick inventory of the supplies you've packed before closing the lid. Did you include everything your child will

need to pass the lunch test successfully? The list should contain eating utensils, plenty of napkins, a drinking cup if required, and a moist towelette for sticky fingers.

Menus

Fortify Fall with the Fun of:

Chicken Darts
Missionary Mustard
Bwana Bites
Jungle Juice

Super Subs
Vita-Greens
Health-Nut Cookies
Fitness Fruit Punch

Cowboy Kabobs
Range Ridin' Relishes
Wild Blueberry Bran Bites
Yahoo Yogurt Drink

Porky Pitas
Light 'n Lemony Sauce
Zucchini Drops
Swiss Soup

Turkey in the Straw
Casper Cut-Outs
Pumpkin Munchkins
Witches' Brew

Thesis on Tuna
Pita Principles
Fieldwork in Fruit
Yogurt 101

Pilgrim's Plate Lunch
Indian Corn Relish
Walnut-Pear Bread
Pumpkin Pleaser

Dippity Sticks
Great Grapes
Souper Sipper
Wheaty Bears

Chicken Taco Cups
Mexicali Sauce
Pancho Villa Veggies
South of the Border Blaster

Tossed-in-a-Tater Salad
Vegetable Cheese Sticks
Fall Fruit Medley
Molasses Cookie

Menus

Chase those Winter Chills with:

Space-Age Sandwich
Blast-Off Broccoli
Astronaut Apples
Mission Control Crunchers

Peanut Butter Jamborees
Skinny Dipped Carrots
Flipped-Out Fruit
Very Vanilla Drink

Baked Potato Soup
Dressed-Up Cucumbers
Nutty Buddy Bites
Fruit Jumble

Vegetable Cheesewiches
Banana Split Salad
Oatmeal Chews
Tomato Teaser

Turkey Wraps
Winter Potato Salad
Apple Crispies
Maple-Nut Yogurt

Ho Ho Hoagies
Vegetable Christmas Tree
Merry Berry Bars
Peppermint Pop

Orient Express Chicken
Sweet-and-Sour Snaps
Far East Carrot Cups
Peking Perk

Ham-It-Up Salad
Waffle Wedges
Three-Fruit Toss
Corny Chowder

Beefy Vegetable Soup
Orange Smiles
Little Dippers
Almond Pudding

Tuna Valentines
Cupid Crunchies
Fudge Kisses
Berries Be Mine

Menus

Sensational Sunny Day menus include:

Turkey and Carrot Salad
Muffin Melbas
Oat Bran Beauties
Fruit Smoothie

Batter Up Chicken
Sell-Out Dipping Sauce
Grand Slam Brownies
Pinch Hitter Punch

Apple Stacks
Super Scoop Veggies
Muncher Muffins
Ginger-Lime Yogurt

Ports Ahoy Tuna
Buccaneer Bread
Meal Maties
Set Sail Spread

Pizza Pies
Da Vinci Vegetables
Pisa Pineapple Skewers
That's Amore Milk

Chick-Pea Salad
Crispy Jicama Critters
Peachy Shortcakes
Milk Malted

Profitable Poultry
Fortune 500 Sauce
14-Carrot Cakes
Millionaire Milk

Chunky Cheese
Bagel Bites
Garden Grazer
Citrus Shake

Barbecue Chicken
Cabbage Slaw
Cornmeal Muffins
Fruit Squeeze

The Asparaguys
Star-Studded Pasta
Broadway Blondies
Symphony in Milk

LUNCHBOX TREATS

120 Recipes for Healthy,
Fun Things to Eat

FALL

Menu

Chicken Darts

Missionary Mustard

Bwana Bites

Jungle Juice

Chicken Darts

4 celery stalks, deveined and cut into 8 sticks (3 inches in length)
8 cherry tomatoes
4 cooked boneless, skinless chicken breasts, cut into 8 triangles
8 four-inch wooden skewers*

This clever main dish is sure to get right to the point of lunchroom conversations.

The day before:
1. Using a paring knife, make several 1-inch cuts on one end of each celery stick.
2. Store in an ice-water bath in the refrigerator. The cut ends of the celery will curl overnight.

Before the school bell rings:
1. Push each wooden skewer through a celery curl, cherry tomato, and chicken triangle.
2. Wrap each dart snugly in plastic. Secure ends with twist ties.
3. Store in the refrigerator until time to travel. Pack 2 Chicken Darts in each lunchbox.

Makes 4 kid-sized servings.

*Recommended for use by children over 5 years of age with adult supervision

Missionary Mustard

1 cup plain low-fat yogurt
1 tablespoon prepared
 mustard
2 teaspoons honey

---

*A zippity-quick dip
for the dart.*

---

1. In a blender jar, combine yogurt, mustard, and honey.
2. Cover. Blend at low speed for 10 seconds or until smooth.
3. Place ¼ cup of the yogurt mixture into each of 4 small plastic containers with snap-on lids.
4. Store in the refrigerator until the car pool is ready to roll.

Makes 4 kid-sized servings.

Bwana Bites

½ cup margarine, melted
½ cup brown sugar
½ cup sugar
3 egg whites
1 cup mashed banana
1 cup all-purpose flour
1 cup whole-wheat flour
¼ teaspoon salt
1 teaspoon baking soda
⅓ cup hot water
⅓ cup chopped pecans

A rich and moist muffin.

1. Preheat oven to 325 degrees. Line 12 regular-size muffin tins with paper baking cups.
2. In a mixing bowl, blend together the melted margarine, sugars, egg whites, and mashed banana.
3. In another bowl, sift all-purpose flour. Measure and then sift again with whole-wheat flour, salt, and baking soda.
4. Alternate adding hot water and dry ingredients to the banana mixture.
5. Spoon batter into paper-lined muffin tins. Top each muffin with a few chopped pecans.
6. Bake 20 minutes or until a toothpick inserted in the center of a muffin comes out with a few crumbs on it. Muffins are moist and the tops may be quite shiny even though the muffin is done.
7. Remove the muffins immediately from the pan. Place them on a wire rack to cool.
8. Wrap each muffin snugly in plastic.
9. Store the whole batch in a gallon-size plastic bag in the refrigerator.

Makes 12 kid-sized servings.

Jungle Juice

1 cup low-fat milk
1 cup pineapple-orange juice
5 tablespoons nonfat dry milk powder

Pack an orange slice and a cherry in the lunchbox to garnish this paradise potion.

---

1. In a blender jar, combine low-fat milk, juice, and milk powder.
2. Cover. Blend at low speed for 10 seconds or until smooth.
3. Pour 1 cup of milk mixture into each of 2 prechilled thermos bottles.
4. Store in the refrigerator until it's time for school.

Makes 2 kid-sized servings.

Menu

Super Subs

Vita-Greens

Health-Nut Cookies

Fitness Fruit Punch

Super Subs

2 eight-inch whole-wheat submarine rolls, halved
3 tablespoons light mayonnaise
2 teaspoons prepared mustard
1½ cups finely chopped 97 percent lean ham
½ cup shredded part-skim mozzarella cheese
½ cup unpeeled fresh apple, chopped

Surprise your superkid with this hearty sandwich.

---

1. Wrap each submarine roll half snugly in plastic. Pack 1 submarine half in each lunchbox.
2. In a mixing bowl, combine the light mayonnaise and mustard. Add the ham, mozzarella cheese, and chopped apple, mixing well.
3. Place ½ cup of the ham mixture into each of 4 small plastic containers with snap-on lids.
4. Store in the refrigerator until time to travel.
5. At lunchtime, stuff each submarine half with ham filling and top with Vita-Greens.

Makes 4 kid-sized servings.

Vita-Greens

1 cup shredded lettuce
1 broccoli stem, washed,
  trimmed, peeled, and cut
  into short julienne strips
  (about ½ cup)
2 carrots, washed, scraped
  and cut into short
  julienne strips (about 1
  cup)

*Fast, fresh, and a great
source of fiber for your
hero's sandwich.*

1. In a small bowl, combine the lettuce, broccoli stems, and julienne-cut carrots, tossing gently.
2. Place ½ cup of the lettuce mixture into each of 4 small plastic containers with snap-on lids.
3. Store in the refrigerator until the car pool is ready to roll.
4. At lunchtime, sprinkle the Vita-Greens on the Super Sub. (Kids give this crunchy sandwich topping higher marks than the traditional lettuce and tomato slice.)

Makes 4 kid-sized servings.

Health-Nut Cookies

½ cup margarine, softened
1 cup brown sugar
⅓ cup nonfat dry milk
  powder
1 egg white
1 teaspoon almond extract
1 cup whole-wheat flour
¾ teaspoon baking soda
¼ teaspoon salt
½ cup butterscotch baking
  chips
2 cups granola cereal
¼ cup raisins

*After-meal cookie treats packed
with granola goodness.*

1. In a mixing bowl, cream the margarine, brown sugar, milk powder, egg white, and almond extract until fluffy.
2. In another bowl, mix together the whole-wheat flour, baking soda, and salt.
3. Combine the dry ingredients with the margarine mixture. Add the butterscotch chips, granola cereal, and raisins.
4. Chill dough in the refrigerator until firm.
5. Preheat oven to 350 degrees.
6. Shape chilled dough into 1½-inch balls. Place 2 inches apart on a baking sheet covered with aluminum foil.
7. Bake 10 to 12 minutes or until cookie tops are lightly browned.
8. Remove cookies from the baking sheet with a metal spatula. Cool to room temperature on wire racks.
9. Store these crunchy cereal treats in quart-size bags in the kitchen pantry.

Makes 18 kid-sized servings.

Fitness Fruit Punch

⅔ cup peach nectar
½ cup plain low-fat yogurt
2 tablespoons nonfat dry
    milk powder
1 cup low-fat milk

*A noontime drink that's sure
to be a lunchroom knockout.*

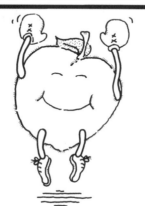

1. In a blender jar, combine nectar, yogurt, milk powder, and low-fat milk.
2. Cover. Blend at low speed for 10 seconds or until smooth.
3. Pour 1 cup of the milk mixture into each of 2 prechilled thermos bottles.
4. Store in the refrigerator until it's time for school.

Makes 2 kid-sized servings.

Menu

Cowboy Kabobs

Range Ridin' Relishes

Wild Blueberry Bran Bites

Yahoo Yogurt Drink

Cowboy Kabobs

8 four-inch wooden
   skewers*
8 one-inch squares farmer
   cheese (½ ounce each)
8 one-inch squares cooked
   turkey breast (½ ounce
   each)
8 black olives

---

*Corral cafeteria appetites with
this high-protein main course.*

---

1. Push each wooden skewer through a square of
farmer cheese, turkey breast
and a black olive.
2. Wrap each kabob snugly
in plastic. Secure ends with
twist ties.
3. Store in the refrigerator
until time to travel. Pack 2
Cowboy Kabobs in each
lunchbox.

Makes 4 kid-sized servings.

*Recommended for use by
children over 5 years of age
with adult supervision

Range Ridin' Relishes

Vegetable relish:
1 medium carrot, thinly
   sliced
1 medium zucchini, sliced
1 cup whole-pod green
   beans, blanched in boiling
   water, refreshed in an ice
   bath, and drained

Marinade:
3 tablespoons olive oil
1 tablespoon white wine
   vinegar
1 tablespoon sugar
Juice of 1 lime

A vegetable relish that's sure to round up some interest from your little cowpokes.

The day before:
1. In a small plastic bowl, combine carrots, zucchini, and green beans. Set aside.
2. In a blender jar, combine olive oil, vinegar, sugar, and lime juice. Cover. Blend at low speed for 10 seconds or until smooth.
3. Pour olive oil mixture over vegetable relishes. Cover with plastic-film wrap. Marinate in the refrigerator overnight.

Before the school bell rings:
1. Place ½ cup of the marinated vegetables into each of 4 small plastic containers with snap-on lids.
2. Store in the refrigerator until the car pool is ready to roll.

Makes 4 kid-sized servings.

Wild Blueberry Bran Bites

2½ cups bran flakes
1 cup low-fat milk
½ cup sugar
½ cup vegetable oil
½ cup honey
½ teaspoon vanilla extract
3 egg whites
1 cup all-purpose flour
⅛ teaspoon salt
1 teaspoon baking soda
½ cup blueberries, drained

There won't be any discouraging words about these fiber-rich treats.

1. Preheat oven to 400 degrees. Line 12 regular-size muffin tins with paper baking cups.
2. In a mixing bowl, combine all ingredients except blueberries.
3. Using an electric mixer, blend at medium speed for 6 minutes.
4. Using a spoon, fold in the drained blueberries.
5. Spoon the batter into paper-lined muffin tins. Bake for 15 minutes or until a toothpick inserted in the center of a muffin comes out clean.
6. Remove muffins immediately from the pan. Place on a wire rack to cool.

7. Wrap each muffin snugly in plastic.
8. Store in a gallon-size plastic bag in the refrigerator.

Makes 12 kid-sized servings.

Yahoo Yogurt Drink

1 eight-ounce container
plain low-fat yogurt
1 cup canned mandarin
oranges, drained
½ cup undiluted evaporated
skimmed milk

*Head 'em out to the playground
with this calcium-fortified drink.*

1. In a blender jar, com-
bine yogurt, mandarin
oranges, and evaporated
milk.
2. Cover. Blend at low
speed for 10 seconds or until smooth.
3. Pour 1 cup of yogurt
mixture into each of 2
prechilled thermos bottles.
4. Store in the refrigerator
until it's time for school.

Makes 2 kid-sized servings.

Menu

Porky Pitas

Light 'n Lemony Sauce

Zucchini Drops

Swiss Soup

Porky Pitas

2 six-inch whole-wheat
  pocket breads
4 lettuce leaves, rinsed and
  drained
1 cup washed, torn raw
  spinach
1 cup diced cooked pork
  loin
1 cup frozen unsweetened
  peach slices, thawed

*The kids will be keen on this
do-it-yourself pocketful of energy.*

1. Halve pocket breads crosswise and wrap each half snugly in plastic. Pack 1 pocket half in each lunchbox.
2. Line 4 small plastic serving containers with lettuce leaves.
3. Layer one quarter of the raw spinach, pork, and peaches in each prepared container.
4. Snap on lid to each container, and store in the refrigerator until time to travel.
5. At lunchtime, fill each pocket half with pork mixture and top with Light 'n Lemony Sauce.

Makes 4 kid-sized servings.

Light 'n Lemony Sauce

1 cup low-fat lemon yogurt
1 teaspoon orange marmalade

A tangy topper perfectly suited for the pita.

---

1. In a blender jar, combine yogurt and marmalade.
2. Cover. Blend at low speed for 10 seconds or until smooth.
3. Place ¼ cup of the yogurt mixture into each of 4 small plastic containers with snap-on lids.
4. Store in the refrigerator until the car pool is ready to roll.

Makes 4 kid-sized servings.

Zucchini Drops

1 cup margarine, softened
¾ cup sugar
1 egg white
½ teaspoon almond extract
1 cup grated unpeeled raw
  zucchini
2 cups whole-wheat flour
½ cup quick-cooking oats
¼ cup wheat germ
1 teaspoon baking powder
1 teaspoon baking soda
1 teaspoon cinnamon
½ cup chopped almonds

*Moist cookies packed with the
fiber of zucchini.*

1. In a mixing bowl, blend together the margarine, sugar, egg white, and almond extract. Stir in the grated zucchini.
2. In another bowl, mix together the whole-wheat flour, oats, wheat germ, baking powder, baking soda, and cinnamon.
3. Combine the dry ingredients with the margarine mixture. Add the chopped almonds.
4. Chill dough in the refrigerator until firm.
5. Preheat oven to 350 degrees.
6. Shape chilled dough into 1½-inch balls. Place 2 inches apart on baking sheet covered with aluminum foil.
7. Bake 10 to 12 minutes or until cookie tops are lightly browned.
8. Remove cookies from the baking sheet with a metal spatula. Cool to room temperature on wire racks.
9. Store these fall favorites in quart-size plastic bags in the kitchen pantry.

Makes 32 kid-sized servings.

Swiss Soup

2 cups low-fat milk
¼ cup prepared low-fat
  beef broth
1 tablespoon cornstarch
1 cup reduced-fat Swiss
  cheese, shredded

An easy cheesy soup.

1. In a medium saucepan over low heat, cook milk for a few minutes until warm but not bubbling.
2. In a small bowl, mix together the beef broth and cornstarch. Pour this mixture into the warm milk.
3. Cook and stir the soup until thick and creamy. Add the cheese. Stir until the cheese melts.
4. Pour 1 cup of the hot soup into each of 2 preheated thermos bottles.

Cook's note: Prepare this showstopping soup just before leaving home to keep it nice and warm for lunch.

Makes 2 kid-sized servings.

Menu

Turkey in the Straw

Casper Cut-Outs

Pumpkin Munchkins

Witches' Brew

Turkey in the Straw

8 one-ounce slices cooked
turkey breast

8 carrots, scraped and cut
into 5-inch sticks

8 twelve-inch pieces of black
string licorice

---

*This snack will sweep you away
with heart-healthy turkey.*

---

1. Fold each slice of turkey
in half lengthwise. Roll
each folded turkey slice
around the end of a carrot
stick.

2. Secure each wrapped
turkey slice on its carrot
handle with a piece of black
string licorice. Tie the ends
of the licorice together in a
knot.

3. Using kitchen scissors,
cut each turkey wrap several times from the bottom to
the top, forming the straw
of a miniature broom.

4. Wrap each Turkey in
the Straw snugly in plastic.
Secure ends with twist ties.

5. Store in the refrigerator
until time to travel. Pack 2

turkey brooms in each
lunchbox.

*Makes 4 kid-
sized servings.*

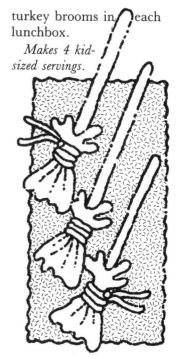

Casper Cut-Outs

4 1½-ounce slices part-skim mozzarella cheese
4 tablespoons black-eyed peas

Calcium-fortified cheese ghosts.

---

1. Using Halloween cookie cutters, cut the cheese slices into goblins. A regular table knife will do the trick if you don't have ghostly cookie cutters.
2. Wrap each cheese goblin snugly in plastic. Set aside.
3. Place 1 tablespoon of black-eyed peas into each of 4 small plastic containers. Children will enjoy conjuring up spooky eyes and bewitching buttons for the cheese goblins with these.
4. Store the Casper Cut-Outs and black-eyed peas in the refrigerator until the car pool is ready to roll.

Makes 4 kid-sized servings.

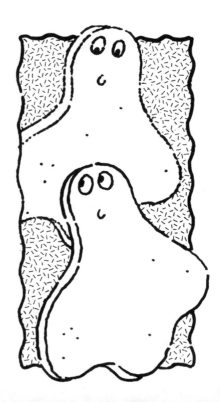

Pumpkin Munchkins

1½ cups brown sugar
2 egg whites
½ cup vegetable oil
1 teaspoon vanilla extract
1 cup cooked mashed
  pumpkin
¼ cup orange juice
2 cups whole-wheat flour
½ cup quick-cooking oats
1 teaspoon baking soda
½ teaspoon salt
1 teaspoon cinnamon
1 tablespoon wheat germ

Whole-wheat flour and orange juice boost the nutrient score of these Halloween sweets.

1. Preheat oven to 350 degrees. Line 12 regular-size muffin tins with paper baking cups.
2. In a mixing bowl, blend together the brown sugar, egg whites, oil, and vanilla. Add the pumpkin and orange juice, blending well.
3. In another bowl, combine whole-wheat flour, oats, baking soda, salt, and cinnamon.
4. Add dry ingredients to the pumpkin mixture, stirring briefly just to moisten.
5. Spoon the batter into paper-lined muffin tins. Top each muffin with wheat germ.
6. Bake for 20 minutes or until a toothpick inserted in the center of a muffin comes out clean.
7. Remove muffins immediately from the pan. Place them on a wire rack to cool.
8. Wrap each muffin snugly in plastic.
9. Store in a gallon-size plastic bag in the refrigerator.

Makes 12 kid-sized servings.

Witches' Brew

2 cups unsweetened apple
  juice
1 cinnamon stick
2 whole cloves

---

*A thirst-quenching drink for
tired little tricksters.*

---

1. In a small saucepan,
combine apple juice, cinnamon stick, and cloves.
2. Cook over medium heat
until mixture boils. Reduce
heat and continue to sim-
mer for 5 minutes.
3. Using a slotted spoon,
remove the cinnamon stick
and cloves.
4. Pour 1 cup of the hot
apple juice into each of 2
preheated thermos bottles.

Cook's note: Prepare this
sorcerer's sipper just before
leaving home to keep it nice
and warm for lunch.

Makes 2 kid-sized servings.

Menu

Thesis on Tuna

Pita Principles

Fieldwork in Fruit

Yogurt 101

Thesis on Tuna

2 cups water-packed solid
  white tuna, drained
⅓ cup sliced black olives
¼ cup chopped celery
1 teaspoon minced onion
2 teaspoons fresh lemon
  juice
3 tablespoons light
  mayonnaise

*A main course in tuna that
takes top honors.*

1. Combine all ingredients
in a medium mixing bowl,
blending well.
2. Place ½ cup of the tuna
mixture into each of 4 plastic containers with snap-on
lids.
3. Store in the refrigerator
until time to travel.
4. At lunchtime, spread the
tuna salad on toasted pita
bread triangles.

Makes 4 kid-sized servings.

Pita Principles

2 six-inch whole-wheat pocket breads
4 teaspoons melted margarine
1 tablespoon grated Parmesan cheese

Skip the class on plain bread and serve up toasted pita triangles.

1. Preheat oven to 425 degrees.
2. Cover a baking sheet (15 × 10 × ½ inch) with aluminum foil. Set aside.
3. Halve each pocket bread crosswise and separate each half into 2 pieces each. Using kitchen scissors, cut each of the 8 single pieces in half, creating a total of 16 triangles.
4. Brush melted margarine on each pita piece. Sprinkle the prepared bread with grated cheese.
5. Arrange seasoned bread triangles on the foil-covered baking sheet.
6. Bake 3 to 5 minutes or until lightly browned and crisp.
7. Store the Pita Principles in quart-size plastic bags in the kitchen pantry.
8. To pack for lunches, wrap 4 pita bread triangles snugly in plastic for each lunchbox.
9. Serve the toasted pita triangles with Thesis on Tuna salad.

Makes 4 kid-sized servings.

Fieldwork in Fruit

1 medium pineapple, peeled, cored, drained, and cut into 1-inch chunks
2 carrots, washed, scraped, and cut into julienne strips (about 1 cup)

Carrots take extra credit in this citrus seminar.

---

1. Place one quarter of the prepared pineapple into each of 4 plastic serving containers.
2. Top each pineapple-filled container with equal portions of carrot.
3. Snap on the lid to each container, and store in the refrigerator until the car pool is ready to roll.

Makes 4 kid-sized servings.

Yogurt 101

2 eight-ounce containers
   plain low-fat yogurt
1 tablespoon honey
Dash of nutmeg

---

*No prerequisites required for this
dairy dessert.*

---

1. In a small mixing bowl, combine yogurt, honey, and nutmeg, mixing well.
2. Spoon 1 cup of the yogurt mixture into each of 2 prechilled plastic containers with snap-on lids.
3. Store in the refrigerator until it's time for school.
4. Don't forget to pack a spoon.

Makes 2 kid-sized servings.

Menu

Pilgrim's Plate Lunch

Indian Corn Relish

Walnut-Pear Bread

Pumpkin Pleaser

Pilgrim's Plate Lunch

4 tablespoons (2 ounces)
   Neufchâtel cheese
⅓ cup plain low-fat yogurt
Pinch of poultry seasoning
1 tablespoon finely chopped
   celery
¼ teaspoon minced onion
1 teaspoon snipped parsley
2 cups diced smoked turkey

A tasty turkey main course.

1. In a small mixing bowl, blend together the cheese and low-fat yogurt until smooth.
2. Stir in the poultry seasoning, celery, onion, and parsley.
3. Add the smoked turkey, mixing well.
4. Place ½ cup of the turkey mixture into each of 4 small plastic containers with snap-on lids.
5. Store in the refrigerator until time to travel.

Makes 4 kid-sized servings.

Indian Corn Relish

2 tablespoons sugar
1 tablespoon cornstarch
2 teaspoons cider vinegar
½ cup apple juice
2 cups canned whole kernel corn, drained
1 tablespoon finely chopped green pepper
1 tablespoon chopped pimiento

A colorful vegetable side dish.

1. In a small saucepan, mix together the sugar and cornstarch. Add vinegar and apple juice, stirring until blended.
2. Cook and stir over low heat until mixture thickens and turns clear.
3. Stir in corn, green pepper, and pimiento.
4. Place ½ cup of the corn mixture into each of 4 small plastic containers with snap-on lids.
5. Store in the refrigerator until the car pool is ready to roll.

Makes 4 kid-sized servings.

Walnut-Pear Bread

Nonstick vegetable spray
1 cup sugar
3 egg whites
½ cup vegetable oil
2 tablespoons plain low-fat
  yogurt
1 teaspoon vanilla extract
2 cups all-purpose flour
1 teaspoon baking soda
½ teaspoon salt
1 cup fresh unpeeled pear,
  chopped
1 cup chopped walnuts

---

*A fruit and nut bread
that brings the entire tribe
to the table*

---

1. Prepare a loaf pan (9 x 5 x 3 inches) with nonstick vegetable spray.
2. Cut wax paper to fit the bottom of the pan. Place carefully into the prepared pan. Set aside.
3. Preheat oven to 350 degrees.
4. In a mixing bowl, combine sugar, egg whites, and vegetable oil. Add yogurt and vanilla extract, blending well.
5. In another bowl, mix together the flour, baking soda, and salt. Add dry ingredients to the yogurt mixture.
6. Stir in the pears and walnuts.

7. Spoon the batter into the prepared loaf pan.
8. Bake 50 minutes or until a toothpick inserted in the center of the bread comes out clean.
9. Remove from oven. Turn bread out of the pan. Cool to room temperature on a wire rack.
10. Wrap the bread snugly in plastic and store in the refrigerator.
11. To pack for lunches, slice the bread into 12 servings and wrap each piece individually.

Makes 12 kid-sized servings.

Pumpkin Pleaser

1 cup cooked mashed
  pumpkin
1½ cups low-fat milk
3 tablespoons nonfat dry
  milk powder
½ teaspoon cinnamon
¼ teaspoon cloves
¼ cup marshmallow cream
4 cinnamon sticks

*A warm drink steaming
with tradition.*

1. In a medium saucepan,
combine pumpkin, low-fat
milk, milk powder, cinna-
mon, and cloves.
2. Cook and stir over low
heat until mixture is hot
but not bubbling.
3. Add marshmallow
cream, blending well.
4. Pour ⅔ cup of hot
pumpkin mixture into each
of 4 preheated thermos
bottles.

Cook's note: Prepare this
Pumpkin Pleaser just before
leaving home to keep it nice
and warm for lunch. Don't
forget to pack a cinnamon
stick stirrer in each
lunchbox.

Makes 4 kid-sized servings.

Menu

Dippity Sticks

Great Grapes

Souper Sipper

Wheaty Bears

Dippity Sticks

8 tablespoons peanut butter
4 six-ounce plastic or paper
  drinking cups
3 medium carrots, scraped
  and cut into 12 sticks
4 three-inch sticks of 97
  percent lean ham (1
  ounce each)
4 three-inch sticks low-fat
  cheddar cheese (1½
  ounces each)

*A protein-packed dip for those
homeroom hungries.*

1. Spoon 2 tablespoons of peanut butter into each of 4 drinking cups.
2. Push 3 carrot sticks, 1 ham stick, and 1 cheese stick into the peanut butter in each cup.
3. Wrap the Dippity Sticks snugly in plastic. Secure with a rubberband around the top of each cup.
4. Store in the refrigerator until time to travel.

Makes 4 kid-sized servings.

Great Grapes

1 cup red seedless grapes
1 cup green seedless grapes

No-fuss, no-muss fruit cup.

1. In a small bowl, combine red grapes and green grapes.
2. Place ½ cup of the grapes into each of 4 small plastic containers with snap-on lids.
3. Store in the refrigerator until the car pool is ready to roll.

Makes 4 kid-sized servings.

Souper Sipper

¼ cup nonfat dry milk powder
1 tablespoon cornstarch
2 teaspoons chicken-flavored instant broth and seasoning mix without MSG.
¼ teaspoon dry mustard
Pinch of white pepper
1½ cups boiling water

A heartwarming addition to any fall menu.

1. In a small mixing bowl with a pour spout, combine all ingredients except water.
2. Add boiling water, stirring constantly until well blended.
3. Pour ¾ cup of the hot soup into each of 2 preheated thermos bottles.
Cook's note: Prepare this sensational sipper just before leaving home to keep it nice and warm for lunch.

Makes 2 kid-sized servings.

Wheaty Bears

1 cup margarine
1 ½ cups brown sugar
2 egg whites
2 teaspoons vanilla extract
1 ½ cups whole-wheat flour
1 cup all-purpose flour
1 teaspoon baking powder
½ teaspoon salt
⅓ cup sugar
½ teaspoon cinnamon

Whole-wheat cookies to round out the meal.

1. In a mixing bowl, blend together the margarine and brown sugar until fluffy. Add the egg whites and vanilla extract, blending well.

2. In another bowl, mix together the whole-wheat flour, all-purpose flour, baking powder, and salt.
3. Combine the dry ingredients with the margarine mixture.
4. Chill the dough in the refrigerator until firm.
5. Preheat oven to 350 degrees.
6. In a small bowl, combine the sugar and cinnamon. Set aside.
7. Work with half of the chilled dough at a time, storing remainder in the refrigerator. Place dough on a lightly floured working surface. Roll out to ⅛-inch thickness.

8. Cut dough with a floured bear-shaped cookie cutter.
9. Place the Wheaty Bears 2 inches apart on baking sheets covered with aluminum foil. Sprinkle with cinnamon sugar mixture.
10. Bake 5 minutes or until cookie edges are lightly browned.
11. Remove Wheaty Bears from baking sheets with a metal spatula. Cool to room temperature on wire racks.
12. Repeat procedure with remaining dough.
13. Store the bears in quart-size plastic bags in the kitchen pantry.
Makes 24 kid-sized servings.

Menu

Chicken Taco Cups

Mexicali Sauce

Pancho Villa Veggies

South of the Border Blaster

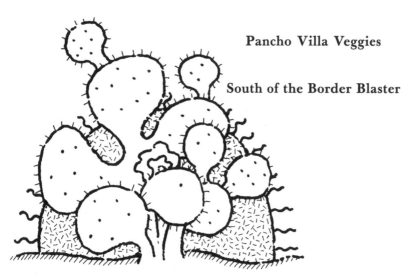

Chicken Taco Cups

4 six-inch whole-wheat tortillas
2 cups diced cooked chicken
½ cup sliced black olives
½ cup cooked, canned kidney beans

A chicken salad that crosses the border in taste.

1. Using a paring knife, make one cut from the center of each tortilla to the outside edge.
2. Place each cut tortilla into a small plastic bowl, overlapping the cut sides to form a cone.
3. Layer one quarter of the chicken, olives, and beans in each prepared bowl.
4. Snap on the lid to each bowl. Store in the refrigerator until time to travel.
5. At lunchtime, top each Chicken Taco Cup with Mexicali Sauce.

Makes 4 kid-sized servings.

Mexicali Sauce

½ cup low-fat cottage
    cheese
½ cup plain low-fat yogurt
1 tablespoon ketchup
⅛ teaspoon cumin
Dash of white pepper

---

*Spicy fiesta flavor in a
smooth sauce.*

---

1. In a blender jar, combine cottage cheese, yogurt, ketchup, cumin, and pepper.
2. Cover. Blend at low speed for 20 seconds or until smooth.
3. Place ¼ cup of the cottage cheese mixture into each of 4 small plastic containers with snap-on lids.
4. Store in the refrigerator until the car pool is ready to roll.
5. Serve with Chicken Taco Cup.

Makes 4 kid-sized servings.

Pancho Villa Veggies

2 large yellow squash, scrubbed, ends removed, and cut into 8 sticks
2 celery stalks, deveined and cut into 8 sticks
1 red bell pepper, seeds removed and cut into 12 strips

A whole bunch of crunch.

1. Place 2 yellow squash sticks, 2 celery sticks, and 3 red bell pepper strips into each of 4 pint-size plastic bags.
2. Drop a few ice cubes in each bag. Close the top. Store in the refrigerator.
3. Don't forget to drain off the water before you pack the snack.

Makes 4 kid-sized servings.

South of the Border Blaster

1 cup unsweetened grape juice

1 cup undiluted evaporated skimmed milk

Grape juice adds a blast of tartness to this beverage.

1. In a plastic pitcher, mix together the grape juice and evaporated milk.
2. Pour 1 cup of the juice mixture into each of 2 prechilled thermos bottles.
3. Store in the refrigerator until it's time for school.

Makes 2 kid-sized servings.

Menu

Tossed-in-a-Tater Salad

Vegetable Cheese Sticks

Fall Fruit Medley

Molasses Cookie

Tossed-in-a-Tater Salad

2 baked potatoes in their
skins
2 cups finely chopped
cooked turkey breast
2 tablespoons sweet pickle
relish
3 tablespoons light
mayonnaise

---

*Baked potatoes contribute
Vitamin C to this mini-meal.*

---

1. Cut each baked potato in
half lengthwise.
2. Scoop out the inside of
each potato half, leaving a
½-inch border of baked
potato around the rim.
Take care not to cut all the
way through the potato
skin.
3. Place each empty potato
shell in a plastic container.
Set aside.
4. In a small mixing bowl,
combine turkey, pickle relish, and light mayonnaise.
5. Carefully spoon ½ cup
of the turkey mixture into
each of the 4 potato shells
in the plastic containers.
Snap on lids.

6. Store the Tossed-in-a-
Tater salads in the refrigerator until time to travel.

Makes 4 kid-sized servings.

Vegetable Cheese Sticks

4 four-inch wooden
 skewers*
12 one-inch squares of part-
 skim mozzarella cheese
 (½ ounce each)
1 medium zucchini, sliced
 into 4 one-inch pieces
4 cherry tomatoes

*Fall vegetables line up in this
satisfying snack.*

1. Push each wooden skewer alternately through a cheese square, a zucchini piece, a cheese square, a cherry tomato, and a cheese square.
2. Wrap each Vegetable Cheese Stick snugly in plastic. Secure ends with twist ties.
3. Store in the refrigerator until you pack the snack.

Makes 4 kid-sized servings.

*Recommended for use by
children over 5 years of age
with adult supervision

Fall Fruit Medley

2 medium oranges, peeled,
   sectioned, and seeded
½ cup black grapes,
   washed, halved length-
   wise, and seeded
1 cup frozen unsweetened
   whole strawberries

---

*This fruit combination is
guaranteed to please.*

---

1. In a small bowl, com-
bine orange sections,
grapes, and frozen straw-
berries. (Don't worry—the
berries will thaw before
lunch.)
2. Place ½ cup of the fruit
combination into each of 4
small plastic containers with
snap-on lids.
3. Store in the refrigerator
until the car pool is ready
to roll.

Makes 4 kid-sized servings.

WE HONK FOR HEALTH!

Molasses Cookie

⅔ cup vegetable oil
1 cup brown sugar
1 egg white
¼ cup molasses
½ teaspoon vanilla extract
1¼ cups whole-wheat flour
1 cup all-purpose flour
2 teaspoons baking soda
½ teaspoon cinnamon
¼ cup sugar

*A cookie that includes
iron-rich molasses.*

1. In a mixing bowl, blend together the vegetable oil and brown sugar. Add the egg white, molasses, and vanilla extract, blending well.
2. In another bowl, mix together the whole-wheat flour, all-purpose flour, baking soda, and cinnamon.
3. Combine the dry ingredients with the molasses mixture.
4. Chill dough in refrigerator until firm.
5. Preheat oven to 350 degrees.
6. Shape chilled dough into 1½-inch balls. Roll each ball in the ¼ cup sugar. Place 2 inches apart on a baking sheet covered with aluminum foil.
7. Bake 10 minutes or until cookie tops are lightly browned.
8. Remove cookies from the baking sheet with a metal spatula. Cool to room temperature on wire racks.
9. Store the munchers in quart-size plastic bags in the kitchen pantry.

Makes 32 kid-sized servings.

Menu

Space Age Sandwich

Blast-Off Broccoli

Astronaut Apples

Mission Control Crunchers

Space-Age Sandwich

4 teaspoons prepared
mustard

8 six-inch whole-wheat tortillas

8 raw spinach leaves

4 two-ounce slices cooked
lean beef, trimmed of fat
before and after cooking

4 1½-ounce slices part-skim
mozzarella cheese

---

*A winning sandwich combination
light-years ahead of its time*

1. Spread 1 teaspoon of
mustard on each of 4
whole-wheat tortillas.
2. Layer each of the 4 prepared tortillas with 2 raw
spinach leaves, a slice of
beef, and a slice of cheese.
Top each with remaining
tortillas.
3. Place each Space-Age
Sandwich between 2 six-
inch paper plates. Wrap
snugly in plastic.
4. Launch lunchroom appe-
tites with supersonic stickers
or your own cosmic crea-
tion written in marker pen
on the paper plate.
5. Store Space-Age Sand-
wiches in the refrigerator
until time to travel.

Makes 4 kid-sized servings.

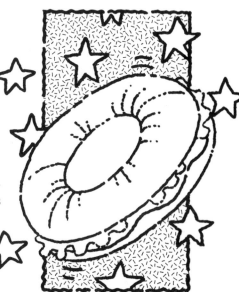

Blast-Off Broccoli

2 cups fresh broccoli florets
½ cup cherry tomatoes,
  halved
¼ cup prepared light
  Italian salad dressing

*Spirits will soar with this
vegetable side dish.*

1. In a small bowl, combine broccoli florets and cherry tomatoes.
2. Pour the salad dressing over the vegetable mixture, tossing to coat.
3. Place ½ cup Blast-Off Broccoli into each of 4 small plastic containers with snap-on lids.
4. Store in the refrigerator until the car pool is ready to roll.

Makes 4 kid-sized servings.

Astronaut Apples

¼ cup fresh lemon juice
1 Granny Smith apple,
  washed, unpeeled, and
  cut into ½-inch cubes
1 Red Delicious apple,
  washed, unpeeled, and
  cut into ½-inch cubes
1 Golden Delicious apple,
  washed, unpeeled, and
  cut into ½-inch cubes
4 tablespoons undiluted
  frozen apple juice concentrate, thawed

Apples make this salad special.

1. In a large mixing bowl, combine the lemon juice with 1 cup of tap water.
2. Place all of the apple cubes in the lemon water, adding more water to cover if necessary.
3. Let the apple cubes soak several minutes. This procedure will keep the apples from turning brown.
4. Drain the apples, discarding the lemon water. Toss the apples gently to mix.
5. Place ½ cup of the apple cubes into each of 4 plastic containers.
6. Spoon 1 tablespoon of juice concentrate over the apples in each container. Snap on lids.
7. Store in the refrigerator until it's time for school.

Makes 4 kid-sized servings.

Mission Control Crunchers

¾ cup margarine
½ cup brown sugar
½ cup sugar
1 teaspoon vanilla extract
¾ cup peanut butter
1 egg white
1 cup all-purpose flour
¾ cup whole-wheat flour
½ teaspoon baking soda
Pinch of salt
½ cup finely chopped un-
salted peanuts

*A sweet surprise for the
cafeteria crew.*

1. In a mixing bowl, blend together the margarine, sugars, and vanilla extract until fluffy. Add the peanut butter and egg white, blending well.
2. In another bowl, mix together the all-purpose flour, whole-wheat flour, baking soda, and salt.
3. Combine the dry ingredients with the peanut butter mixture. Add the chopped peanuts.
4. Chill dough in the refrigerator until firm.
5. Preheat oven to 350 degrees.
6. Shape chilled dough into 1½-inch balls. Place 2 inches apart on a baking sheet covered with aluminum foil.
7. Bake 10 minutes or until cookie tops are lightly browned.
8. Remove cookies from the baking sheet with a metal spatula. Cool to room temperature on wire racks.
9. Store Crunchers in quart-size plastic bags in the kitchen pantry.

Makes 32 kid-sized servings.

Menu

Peanut Butter Jamborees

Skinny Dipped Carrots

Flipped-Out Fruit

Very Vanilla Drink

Peanut Butter Jamborees

Peanut butter bread:

Nonstick vegetable spray
½ cup unsalted peanut
  butter
2 tablespoons honey
1 cup orange juice
1 egg white
⅓ cup brown sugar
1 teaspoon vanilla extract
2 cups whole-wheat flour
½ teaspoon salt
1 tablespoon baking powder

---

*How to build a better peanut
butter–and-jelly sandwich.*

Jamborees:

4 teaspoons apricot jam
4 two-ounce slices cooked
  turkey breast

To prepare bread:

1. Preheat oven to 350
degrees. Prepare a loaf pan
(9 x 5 x 3 inches) with nonstick vegetable spray. Line
the bottom of the prepared
pan with wax paper. Set
aside.
2. In a mixing bowl, blend
together the peanut butter
and honey. Add the orange
juice, egg white, brown
sugar, and vanilla extract,
blending well.
3. In another bowl, mix
together whole-wheat flour,
salt, and baking powder.
4. Combine wet and dry
ingredients, mixing briefly
to moisten.

5. Spoon batter into the prepared loaf pan. Bake for 30 minutes or until toothpick inserted in the center of the bread comes out clean. Remove from oven.

6. Turn bread out of pan and cool on wire rack.

7. Cut the bread into 10 slices. Wrap snugly in plastic and store in the refrigerator.

To assemble Jamborees:

1. Spread 1 teaspoon of apricot jam on each of 5 slices of the peanut butter bread.

2. Place a slice of cooked turkey breast on each prepared slice of bread.

3. Top with another slice of peanut butter bread.

4. Wrap each Peanut Butter Jamboree snugly in plastic.

5. Store in the refrigerator until just before the school bell rings.

Makes 5 kid-sized servings.

Skinny Dipped Carrots

Carrot sticks:
4 medium carrots, scraped
   and cut into 16 sticks

Skinny dip:
1 cup low-fat ricotta cheese
½ cup frozen chopped
   broccoli, thawed

---

*Simple and satisfying, this side
dish also makes a tasty snack.*

To assemble carrot sticks:
1. Place 4 carrot sticks into
each of 4 pint-size plastic
bags.
2. Drop a few ice cubes in
each bag. Close the top.
Store in the refrigerator.
Drain off water when ready
to pack the snack.

To prepare dip:
1. In a blender jar, com-
bine the ricotta cheese and
chopped broccoli.
2. Cover. Blend at low
speed for 2 minutes or until
smooth.
3. Place ¼ cup of cheese
mixture into each of 4 small
plastic containers with snap-
on lids.

4. Store in the refrigerator
until time to travel.

Makes 4 kid-sized servings.

Flipped-Out Fruit

¼ cup washed red seedless grapes, halved

¼ cup pineapple tidbits, well drained

4 Granny Smith apples, washed

Bowl them over with a crazy fruit cup.

1. In a small bowl, combine grapes and pineapple tidbits. Set aside.

2. Using a paring knife, slice off the top of each apple. Save the tops. You will need them later to serve as lids for the apple bowls.

3. Core each apple to within ½ inch of the bottom, taking care not to cut all the way through.

4. Scoop out each cavity to make a little bowl about 1½ inches across.

5. Fill each bowl with 2 tablespoons of the fruit mixture. Top each apple bowl with its lid.

6. Wrap each apple snugly in plastic.

7. Store in the refrigerator until the car pool is ready to roll.

Makes 4 kid-sized servings.

Very Vanilla Drink

1 eight-ounce container low-
  fat vanilla yogurt
1 cup low-fat milk

---

*A just-right refresher rich enough
to serve as dessert.*

---

1. In a blender jar, combine vanilla yogurt and low-fat milk.
2. Cover. Blend at low speed for 10 seconds or until smooth.
3. Pour 1 cup of yogurt mixture into each of 2 prechilled thermos bottles.
4. Store in the refrigerator until it's time for school.

Makes 2 kid-sized servings.

Menu

Baked Potato Soup

Dressed-Up Cucumbers

Nutty Buddy Bites

Fruit Jumble

Baked Potato Soup

1 cup prepared low-fat chicken broth

1 cup low-fat milk

⅔ cup instant mashed potato flakes

1 cup finely chopped 97 percent lean ham

½ cup shredded low-fat cheddar cheese

A tasty soup to cure wintertime lunchbox blues.

---

1. In a small saucepan, bring chicken broth to a boil.

2. Reduce heat and stir in low-fat milk until mixture simmers.

3. Sprinkle instant mashed potato flakes over the milk mixture, stirring constantly. Add ham and shredded cheese. Continue to simmer and stir just until soup is heated through and cheese begins to melt. Do not boil.

4. Pour 1 cup of the hot soup into each of 2 preheated thermos bottles.

Cook's note: This recipe works only if the directions are followed to the letter.

Be sure to stir it up quickly, load it into the preheated thermos just before leaving home, and, oh, yes, pack a spoon for scooping.

Makes 2 kid-sized servings.

Dressed-Up Cucumbers

2 cucumbers, peeled, seeded, and cut into 8 spears

Dressing:
1 tablespoon sugar
2 tablespoons ketchup
1 teaspoon cider vinegar
1 teaspoon fresh lime juice
Pinch of paprika
Pinch of white pepper
3 tablespoons vegetable oil

*Charge up cucumbers with this
colorful homemade dressing.*

1. In a food processor,
combine sugar, ketchup,
vinegar, lime juice, paprika,
and white pepper.
2. Blend at low speed until
smooth. Add oil, 1 table-
spoon at a time, blending
after each addition, to make
salad dressing.
3. In a medium bowl, mix
together salad dressing and
cucumber spears.
4. Place 2 Dressed-Up Cu-
cumber spears in each of 4
small plastic containers with
snap-on lids.
5. Store in the refrigerator
until you pack the snack.

Makes 4 kid-sized servings.

Nutty Buddy Bites

½ cup natural wheat and barley cereal

1 cup buttermilk made from low-fat milk

1 cup brown sugar

1 tablespoon molasses

1 egg white

1 teaspoon vanilla extract

1 cup whole-wheat flour

¾ cup all-purpose flour

½ teaspoon baking soda

1 teaspoon baking powder

¼ teaspoon salt

These chewy morsels also make a great after-school snack.

---

1. Preheat oven to 350 degrees. Line 36 minimuffin tins with paper baking cups.

2. In a small bowl, combine the wheat and barley cereal and buttermilk. Set aside for 10 minutes.

3. In a mixing bowl, blend together the brown sugar, molasses, egg white, and vanilla extract. Add the cereal mixture, blending well.

4. In another bowl, mix together the whole-wheat flour, all-purpose flour, baking soda, baking powder, and salt.

5. Stir the dry ingredients into the cereal mixture.

6. Spoon batter into paper-lined minimuffin tins. Bake for 10 minutes or until a toothpick inserted in the center of a muffin comes out clean.

7. Remove muffins immediately from the pan. Place them on a wire rack to cool.

8. Wrap each little muffin snugly in plastic.

9. Store the whole batch in a gallon-size plastic bag in the kitchen pantry. Pack 3 Nutty Buddy Bites in each lunchbox when the car pool is ready to roll.

Makes 12 kid-sized servings.

Fruit
Jumble

1 cup canned pineapple
chunks, packed in juice
1 small banana, peeled and
sliced
1 firm ripe pear, washed,
unpeeled, cored, and
sliced into chunks

*A chunky winter salad chock-
full of vitamin C.*

1. In a small bowl, com-
bine pineapple chunks,
banana slices, and pear
chunks, tossing gently.
2. Place ½ cup of the fruit
mixture into each of 4 small
plastic containers with snap-
on lids.
3. Store in the refrigerator
until it's time for school.

Makes 4 kid-sized servings.

Menu

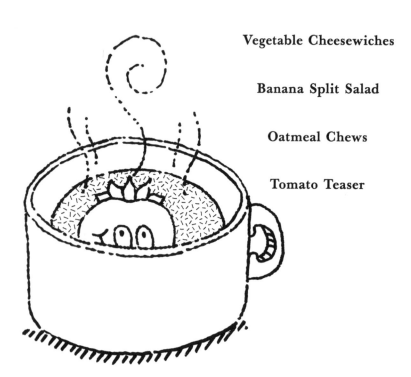

Vegetable Cheesewiches

Banana Split Salad

Oatmeal Chews

Tomato Teaser

Vegetable Cheesewiches

8 slices homestyle whole-grain bread
1½ cups shredded part-skim mozzarella cheese
½ cup grated carrots
¼ cup light mayonnaise

This neat-to-eat sandwich is vitamin fortified.

---

1. Using a cookie cutter, cut the bread slices into circles.
2. Divide the 8 bread circles into 4 stacks of 2.
3. Wrap each of the 4 stacks snugly in plastic. Pack 1 bread stack in each lunchbox.
4. In a small mixing bowl, combine mozzarella cheese, grated carrots, and light mayonnaise.
5. Place ¼ cup of the cheese mixture into each of 4 small plastic containers with snap-on lids.
6. Store in the refrigerator until time to travel.
7. At lunchtime, spread cheese filling on each whole-wheat circle.

Makes 4 kid-sized servings.

Banana Split Salad

4 ripe medium bananas,
unpeeled
¼ cup orange juice
½ cup canned mandarin
oranges, drained (16 in-
dividual sections)

An "a-peeling" fruit salad.

1. Using a paring knife,
split each banana length-
wise, taking care not to cut
through the peel on the op-
posite side.
2. Brush the inside of each
split banana with orange
juice, to help keep the
banana from turning dark.
3. Carefully place 4 mandarin orange sections in each
split banana.
4. Wrap each Banana Split
Salad in aluminum foil.
Twist the ends to seal.

Cook's Note: Prepare this
salad just before serving; no
need to refrigerate. Pack a
spoon.

Makes 4 kid-sized servings.

Oatmeal Chews

½ cup margarine
1 cup brown sugar
2 egg whites
1 teaspoon vanilla extract
1 cup whole-wheat flour
½ teaspoon baking soda
¼ teaspoon salt
¼ teaspoon baking powder
1 cup quick-cooking oats
½ cup peanut butter chips
¼ cup natural wheat and
   barley cereal

A chewy cookie with a surprising crunch tucked inside.

1. In a mixing bowl, blend together the margarine, brown sugar, egg whites, and vanilla extract.
2. In another bowl, mix together the whole-wheat flour, baking soda, salt, baking powder, and oats.
3. Combine the dry ingredients with the margarine mixture. Stir in the peanut butter chips and cereal.
4. Chill the dough in the refrigerator until firm.
5. Preheat the oven to 350 degrees.
6. Shape chilled dough into 1½-inch balls. Place 2 inches apart on a baking sheet covered with aluminum foil.
7. Bake 8 to 10 minutes or until cookie tops are lightly browned.
8. Remove cookies from the baking sheet with a metal spatula. Cool to room temperature on wire racks.
9. Store the crispy cereal treats in quart-size plastic bags in the kitchen pantry.

Makes 24 kid-sized servings.

Tomato Teaser

1 cup 100 percent vegetable
juice with no added salt
1 cup prepared low-fat beef
broth

*This spicy drink can add a
warm glow to a cold lunch.*

1. In a small saucepan,
combine vegetable juice and
beef broth.
2. Cook over medium heat
until hot.
3. Pour 1 cup of the hot
vegetable drink into each of
2 preheated thermos bottles.

Cook's note: Prepare just
before leaving home to keep
this drink nice and warm
for lunch.

Makes 2 kid-sized servings.

Menu

Turkey Wraps

Winter Potato Salad

Apple Crispies

Maple-Nut Yogurt

Turkey Wraps

½ cup plain low-fat yogurt
2 teaspoons ketchup
1 teaspoon sweet pickle relish
8 one-ounce slices cooked turkey breast
8 five-inch breadsticks

Easy-to-pack protein with a surprise center.

---

1. In a small bowl, mix together the low-fat yogurt, ketchup, and relish. Set aside.
2. Cover a smooth working surface with waxed paper. Place the 8 slices of turkey breast side by side on the prepared working surface.
3. Spoon 1 tablespoon of the yogurt mixture on each turkey slice.
4. Lay a breadstick on each prepared turkey slice. Roll each turkey slice around a breadstick.
5. Enclose each Turkey Wrap snugly in plastic. Secure ends with twist ties.
6. Store in the refrigerator until time to travel. Pack 2 Turkey Wraps in each lunchbox.

Makes 4 kid-sized servings.

Winter Potato Salad

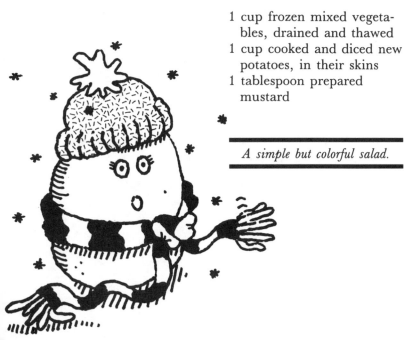

1 cup frozen mixed vegetables, drained and thawed
1 cup cooked and diced new
potatoes, in their skins
1 tablespoon prepared
mustard

A simple but colorful salad.

1. In a small mixing bowl,
combine the vegetables,
new potatoes, and mustard,
tossing well.
2. Spoon ½ cup of the
vegetable mixture into each
of 4 plastic containers with
snap-on lids.
3. Store in the refrigerator
until you pack the snack.

Makes 4 kid-sized servings.

Apple Crispies

Nonstick vegetable spray
6 cups peeled, thinly sliced
  apples
½ cup brown sugar
¼ cup margarine
2 cups toasted rice cereal

A no-fuss fruit-and-fiber dessert.

1. Preheat the oven to 350 degrees. Prepare a baking pan (8 × 8 × 2 inches) with nonstick vegetable spray.
2. Spread the apples evenly in the prepared baking pan.
3. In a mixing bowl, combine brown sugar and margarine with a pastry blender until crumbly.
4. Using a wooden spoon, stir the cereal into the margarine mixture.
5. Sprinkle the cereal topping over the apples.
6. Bake for 20 minutes or until apples are tender and topping is lightly browned.

7. Remove pan from the oven. Place on a wire rack to cool.
8. Place 1/2 cup of Apple Crispies in each of 6 small plastic containers with snap-on lids.
9. Store in the refrigerator until the car pool is ready to roll.

Makes 6 kid-sized servings.

Maple-Nut Yogurt

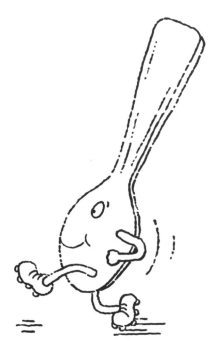

2 eight-ounce containers plain low-fat yogurt
2 teaspoons maple syrup
2 teaspoons chopped toasted pecans

Dressed-up yogurt completes the meal.

1. In a small mixing bowl, combine yogurt, maple syrup, and toasted pecans, mixing well.
2. Spoon 1 cup of the yogurt mixture into each of 2 chilled plastic containers with snap-on lids.
3. Store in the refrigerator until it's time for school.

Cook's note: Don't forget to pack a spoon.

Makes 2 kid-sized servings.

Menu

Ho Ho Hoagies

Vegetable Christmas Tree

Merry Berry Bars

Peppermint Pop

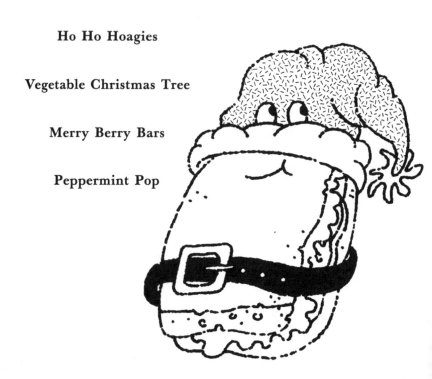

Ho Ho Hoagies

1 twelve-inch loaf of French bread

2 tablespoons prepared mustard

2 cups cooked and diced pork loin

½ red bell pepper, seeds removed and cut into chunks

½ yellow bell pepper, seeds removed and cut into chunks

1 cup mixed salad greens

4 twelve-inch pieces of red string licorice

A pork-filled hoagie with colorful trimmings.

---

1. Slice the loaf of French bread in half lengthwise. Spread the inside of the top half with 1 tablespoon of the mustard. Set aside.

2. Using a spoon, scoop out the inside of the bottom half, forming a shallow well. Spread the inside of the bread shell with the remaining 1 tablespoon of mustard.

3. Layer the pork, red pepper, and yellow pepper in the prepared bread shell. Top with the mixed salad greens. Cover with the remaining French bread half.

4. Cut the filled French loaf into 4 little hoagies, each about 3 inches long.

5. Wrap a red licorice string around each portion. Tie the ends of the licorice together in a bow on the top of each hoagie.

6. Seal each hoagie snugly in plastic.

7. Store in the refrigerator until time to travel. Pack 1 hoagie in each lunchbox.

Makes 4 kid-sized servings.

Vegetable Christmas Tree

1 tablespoon prepared buttermilk salad dressing
4 tablespoons plain low-fat
yogurt
6 trimmed broccoli florets
A 1½-inch carrot stem end,
washed and scraped
1 cherry tomato
⅔ cup cauliflower pieces

---

*Wrap up this winter vegetable
salad in your lunchbox.*

---

1. In a small mixing bowl, combine salad dressing and cottage cheese, mixing well.
2. Using a spatula, spread the prepared dressing over the bottom of a square plastic sandwich container (5 × 5 × 1 inch).
3. On the dressing, create a winter wonderland by carefully arranging the broccoli florets in the shape of a pine tree, with the carrot stem as the tree base, the tomato as a treetop orna-ment, and the cauliflower as snow.
4. Cut a square of plastic bubble packing material (5 × 5 inches) to fit the container. Place it over the winter vegetable arrange-ment. Snap on the lid to the plastic container.
5. Store in the refrigerator until time for sleigh bells to jingle. The plastic bubble pack will keep the Vegetable Christmas Tree intact dur-ing travel.
6. Be sure to invite a friend to lunch. This snack pro-vides enough crunching to share.

Makes 2 kid-sized servings.

Merry Berry Bars

Nonstick vegetable spray
Apple filling:
½ cup sugar
2 tablespoons cornstarch
½ teaspoon cinnamon
2 tablespoons apple juice
2 cups unpeeled and
  chopped apple
1 cup canned whole-berry
  cranberry sauce

*Cranberry and apple pie bars
that add a twist to tradition.*

Crust:
⅓ cup margarine
½ cup brown sugar
1 egg white
1 cup all-purpose flour
1 cup whole-wheat flour
1 teaspoon baking powder
½ teaspoon salt
Crumb topping:
⅓ cup margarine
½ cup brown sugar
½ cup whole-wheat flour
½ cup quick-cooking oats
¼ cup finely chopped
  pecans

1. Prepare a baking pan (9
× 13 × 2 inches) with
nonstick vegetable spray.
Set aside.

To prepare apple filling:
2. In a medium saucepan,
combine 1/2 cup sugar,
cornstarch, cinnamon, and
apple juice.
3. Add apples and cranberry sauce. Cook and stir
over low heat until thick-
ened. Set aside to cool com-
pletely.

To prepare crust:
4. In a mixing bowl, cream
together ⅓ cup margarine
and ½ cup brown sugar.
Add the egg white, blending
well.
5. In another bowl, mix
together the all-purpose
flour, whole-wheat flour,
baking powder, and salt.

6. Combine wet and dry ingredients, stirring until well mixed. Pat the dough evenly into the prepared pan, pressing it about half-way up the sides.
7. Preheat the oven to 350 degrees.

To prepare crumb topping:
8. In a small bowl, mix ⅓ cup margarine, ½ cup brown sugar, ½ cup whole-wheat flour, quick-cooking oats, and chopped pecans. Blend with your hands until mixture is crumbly.
9. Spread cooled apple filling over the dough in the prepared pan. Sprinkle the crumb topping over the filling.
10. Bake for 30 minutes or until top is lightly browned. Remove from oven and place on wire rack to cool.
11. Wrap the pan of Merry Berry Bars snugly in plastic and store in the refrigerator.
12. To pack for lunches, slice into 24 bars and wrap each piece individually. Place 1 bar in each lunchbox.

Makes 24 kid-sized servings.

Peppermint Pop

2 cups low-fat milk
3 tablespoons nonfat dry
  milk powder
⅛ teaspoon peppermint
  extract
½ cup frozen unsweetened
  strawberries
2 peppermint sticks

---

*Add a splash of spirit with
this seasonal drink.*

---

1. In a blender jar, combine low-fat milk, milk powder, peppermint extract, and frozen strawberries.
2. Cover. Blend at low speed for 15 seconds or until smooth.
3. Transfer the milk mixture to a medium saucepan. Heat at low temperature until hot but not simmering.
4. Pour 1 cup of hot milk mixture into each of 2 preheated thermos bottles.

Cook's note: Prepare Peppermint Pop just before leaving home to keep it nice and warm for lunch. For a special touch add a peppermint stick to each lunchbox for a super straw.

*Makes 2
kid-sized servings.*

Menu

Orient Express Chicken

Sweet-and-Sour Snaps

Far East Carrot Cups

Peking Perk

Orient Express Chicken

2 cups diced cooked chicken
¼ cup thinly sliced water
   chestnuts
½ cup canned pineapple
   chunks, drained
3 tablespoons light
   mayonnaise

*Stir up this main-dish salad
in no time.*

1. In a medium bowl, combine chicken, water chestnuts, and pineapple chunks.
2. Add salad dressing to the chicken mixture, blending well.
3. Place ½ cup of Orient Express Chicken into each of 4 small plastic containers with snap-on lids.
4. Store in the refrigerator until time to travel.

Makes 4 kid-sized servings.

Sweet-and-Sour Snaps

Snaps:
24 Chinese pea pods
Sweet-and-sour sauce:
1 cup low-fat ricotta cheese
2 teaspoons fresh lemon
juice
1 tablespoon orange mar-
malade

Vegetable delicacies in a snap.

To assemble snaps:
1. Place 6 pea pods into
each of 4 pint-size plastic
bags.
2. Drop a few ice cubes in
each bag. Close the top.
Store in the refrigerator.
3. Don't forget to drain off
the water before you pack
the snack.

**To prepare sweet-and-sour
sauce:**
1. In a blender jar, com-
bine ricotta cheese, lemon
juice, and orange mar-
malade.
2. Cover. Blend at low
speed for 1 minute or until
smooth.

3. Place ¼ cup of sauce
into each of 4 small plastic
containers with snap-on
lids.
4. Store in the refrigerator
until car pool is ready to
roll.
5. At lunchtime, dip the
snaps in the sauce.

Makes 4 kid-sized servings.

118

Far East Carrot Cups

1 cup brown sugar
½ cup sugar
2 egg whites
½ cup vegetable oil
1 teaspoon vanilla extract
1 cup cooked, mashed
  carrots
¼ cup apple juice
2 cups whole-wheat flour
½ cup quick-cooking oats
1 teaspoon baking soda
½ teaspoon salt
½ teaspoon cinnamon
¼ teaspoon ginger

A most honorable muffin.

1. Preheat oven to 350 degrees. Line 12 regular-size muffin tins with paper baking cups.
2. In a mixing bowl, blend together the sugars, egg whites, oil, and vanilla extract. Add the carrots and apple juice, blending well.
3. In another bowl, mix together the whole-wheat flour, oats, baking soda, salt, cinnamon, and ginger.
4. Combine the dry ingredients with the carrot mixture, stirring just to moisten.
5. Spoon the batter into the paper-lined muffin tins.
6. Bake for 20 minutes or until a toothpick inserted in the center of a muffin comes out clean.
7. Remove muffins immediately from the pan. Place them on a wire rack to cool.
8. Wrap each muffin snugly in plastic.
9. Store the whole batch in a gallon-size plastic bag in the refrigerator.

Makes 12 kid-sized servings.

Peking Perk

1 eight-ounce container
  plain low-fat yogurt
1 cup low-fat milk
¼ teaspoon almond extract
2 teaspoons honey

*Nutty, sweet flavor
in a cool drink.*

1. In a blender jar, combine yogurt, milk, almond extract, and honey.
2. Cover. Blend at low speed for 10 seconds or until smooth.
3. Pour 1 cup of yogurt mixture into each of 2 prechilled thermos bottles.
4. Store in the refrigerator until time for school.

Makes 2 kid-sized servings.

Menu

Ham-It-Up Salad

Waffle Wedges

Three-Fruit Toss

Corny Chowder

Ham-It-Up Salad

2 cups diced 97 percent
    lean ham
½ cup frozen cut green be-
    ans, thawed and drained
½ cup bite-size cauliflower
    pieces
¼ cup plain low-fat yogurt
2 tablespoons prepared but-
    termilk salad dressing

Ham it up for the holidays with
this untraditional winter salad.

1. In a medium bowl, com-
bine ham, green beans,
cauliflower, yogurt, and
salad dressing.
2. Place ¾ cup of the ham
mixture into each of 4 small
plastic containers with snap-
on lids.
3. Store in the refrigerator
until time to travel.
4. At lunchtime, spread
Ham-It-Up Salad over
Waffle Wedges.

Makes 4 kid-sized servings.

Waffle Wedges

1 cup all-purpose flour
½ teaspoon salt
2 teaspoons baking powder
1 cup low-fat milk
¼ cup vegetable oil
1 cup shredded low-fat
  cheddar cheese
2 egg whites

---

*Shredded cheese adds
new flavor to this waffle.*

---

1. Sift together the flour, salt, and baking powder. Set aside.
2. In a mixing bowl, combine the milk, vegetable oil, and cheese. Add the dry ingredients.
3. In another bowl, beat the egg whites until stiff but not dry. Fold into the batter.
4. Bake in the waffle iron following manufacturer's directions.
5. To pack for lunches, divide each waffle into quarters. Wrap each quarter snugly in plastic. Pack 2 quarters, or wedges, into each lunchbox.
6. Serve with Ham-It-Up Salad.

Makes 6 kid-sized servings.

Three-Fruit Toss

1 Ruby Red grapefruit, peeled and sectioned
1 white grapefruit, peeled and sectioned
2 oranges, peeled, sectioned, and pith discarded

Citrus fruit brings out the sunshine on cold and gray winter days.

---

1. In a small bowl, combine the grapefruit and orange sections.
2. Place ½ cup of the fruit mixture into each of 4 small plastic containers with snap-on lids.
3. Store in the refrigerator until the car pool is ready to roll.

Makes 4 kid-sized servings.

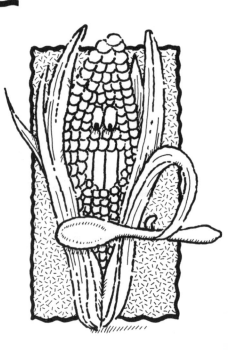

Corny Chowder

Nonstick vegetable spray
½ cup whole kernel corn
¼ cup onion, finely
   chopped
¼ cup celery, finely
   chopped
2 cups low-fat milk
¼ cup prepared low-fat
   chicken broth
1 tablespoon cornstarch

---

*A winter warm-up soup spooned
from a thermos cup.*

---

1. Prepare a medium
saucepan with nonstick
vegetable spray. Add whole
kernel corn, chopped onion,
and chopped celery. Sauté
over low heat for 1 minute
or until vegetables are fork
tender.
2. Stir in the milk. Con-
tinue to cook over low heat
for several minutes until the
milk mixture is hot but not
simmering.
3. In a small bowl, mix
together the chicken broth
and cornstarch using a
small rubber spatula. Pour
into the milk mixture.
4. Cook and stir the soup
until it is thick and creamy.

5. Pour 1 cup of the hot
soup into each of 2 preheated thermos bottles.

Cook's note: Prepare this
chill-chaser just before leaving home to keep it nice
and warm for lunch. You'll
need a spoon to celebrate
with this soup.

Makes 2 kid-sized servings.

Menu

Beefy Vegetable Soup

Orange Smiles

Little Dippers

Almond Pudding

Beefy Vegetable Soup

1 cup 100 percent vegetable juice with no added salt
½ cup prepared low-fat beef broth
4 teaspoons cornstarch
1 cup finely chopped, cooked lean beef, trimmed of fat
1 cup frozen mixed vegetables, thawed

A hearty soup that can be prepared from leftovers.

1. Place the vegetable juice in a medium saucepan. Cook over low heat for a few minutes until the juice is hot but not boiling.
2. In a small bowl, mix together the beef broth and cornstarch using a small rubber spatula. Stir the mixture into the heated vegetable juice.
3. Cook and stir over low heat until broth mixture thickens.
4. Add cooked beef and mixed vegetables. Continue to cook until all ingredients are thoroughly heated.
5. Pour 1 cup of the hot soup into each of 2 preheated thermos bottles.

Cook's note: Prepare this sipper just before leaving home to keep it nice and warm for lunch. Toss a spoon into the lunchbox.

Makes 2 kid-sized servings.

Orange Smiles

4 fresh oranges

Round out winter menus with these simple-to-make and easy-to-take fruit treats.

1. Place the oranges on a smooth working surface.
2. Draw a happy face on each orange with a marker or writing pen.
3. Using a zester, a carrot peeler, or a small paring knife, gently carve into the rind of the orange following the pattern made with the marker.
4. When each Orange Smile is complete, wrap it snugly in plastic wrap. Use twist ties to secure the ends.
5. Store in the refrigerator until the car pool is ready to roll. Pack 1 Orange Smile in each lunchbox.

Makes 4 kid-sized servings.

Little Dippers

Nonstick vegetable spray
1 cup all-purpose flour
1 cup graham cracker
  crumbs
½ cup whole-wheat flour
2 teaspoons baking powder
½ teaspoon baking soda
½ teaspoon salt
½ teaspoon cinnamon
1 egg white
⅓ cup honey
1 cup low-fat milk
3 tablespoons vegetable oil
1 teaspoon vanilla extract

*A wholesome bread that is also
a dipper for soup.*

1. Prepare a loaf pan (9 ×
5 × 3 inches) with nonstick
vegetable spray and line
with waxed paper.
2. Preheat the oven to 350
degrees.
3. In a mixing bowl, com-
bine flour, graham cracker
crumbs, whole-wheat flour,
baking powder, baking
soda, salt, and cinnamon.
4. Add the egg white,
honey, milk, vegetable oil,
and vanilla extract to the
flour mixture, stirring just
until dry ingredients are
moistened.
5. Spoon the batter into the
prepared loaf pan.
6. Bake 35 minutes or until
a toothpick inserted in the

center of the bread comes
out clean.
7. Remove from the oven.
Turn the bread out of the
pan. Cool to room temperature on a wire rack.
8. Wrap the bread snugly
in plastic and store in the
refrigerator.
9. To pack for lunches,
slice the bread into 12 Little
Dippers and wrap each
piece individually.

Makes 12 kid-sized servings.

Almond Pudding

⅓ cup sugar
3 tablespoons cornstarch
2½ cups low-fat milk
1 teaspoon almond extract
3 tablespoons toasted
  blanched slivered almonds

Almonds add a gourmet touch to this simple pudding.

1. In a medium saucepan, mix together the sugar and cornstarch. Add milk, blending well.
2. Stirring constantly, cook the milk mixture over low heat until it thickens.
3. Remove the pudding from the heat. Add the almond extract, blending well.
4. Place 1 cup of pudding into each of 3 plastic containers. Top each serving with a tablespoon of toasted almonds. Snap on lids.
5. Store in the refrigerator until it's time for school.

Cook's note: The trick in preparing any homemade pudding is to stir it constantly. Your undivided attention will prevent both lumpiness and scorching.

Makes 3 kid-sized servings.

Menu

Tuna Valentines

Cupid Crunchies

Fudge Kisses

Berries Be Mine

Tuna Valentines

8 slices homestyle whole-
wheat bread, cut into
heart shapes
2 cups water-packed solid
white tuna, drained
½ cup canned crushed
pineapple, drained
2 tablespoons light
mayonnaise

---

*Tuna makes a hearty Valentine
sandwich treat.*

---

1. Divide the 8 bread
hearts into 4 stacks of 2.
2. Wrap each of the 4
stacks snugly in plastic.
Pack 1 bread stack in each
lunchbox.
3. In a mixing bowl, com-
bine tuna, pineapple, and
light mayonnaise.
4. Place ½ cup of the tuna
mixture into each of 4 small
plastic containers with snap-
on lids.
5. Store in the refrigerator
until time to travel.
6. At lunchtime, spread
tuna filling on each whole-
wheat heart.
7. Be sure to add a Valentine from the cook.

Makes 4 kid-sized servings.

Cupid Crunchies

Crunchies:
3 medium carrots, scraped and cut into 12 sticks
2 small zucchini squash, cut into 8 sticks
Heart-smart dip:
1 cup low-fat cottage cheese
½ teaspoon sodium-free lemon herb seasoning
2 tablespoons low-fat buttermilk

Crunchy snacks with a vegetable dip the kids can eat to their heart's content.

To assemble crunchies:
1. Place 3 carrot sticks and 2 zucchini sticks into each of 4 pint-size plastic bags.
2. Drop a few ice cubes in each bag. Close the top. Store in the refrigerator until ready to pack the snack. Drain before packing.

To prepare dip:
1. In a blender jar, combine cottage cheese, seasoning, and buttermilk.
2. Cover. Blend at low speed for 15 seconds or until smooth.
3. Place ¼ cup of the cottage cheese mixture into each of 4 small plastic containers with snap-on lids.
4. Store in the refrigerator until the car pool is ready to roll.

Makes 4 kid-sized servings.

Fudge Kisses

3 ounces semisweet
   chocolate
½ cup margarine
¾ cup sugar
½ cup whole-wheat flour
3 egg whites
1 teaspoon vanilla extract

Miniature fudgy desserts.

---

1. Preheat the oven to 325 degrees. Line 24 minimuffin tins with paper baking cups. (Foil cups will dress up the treats for special occasions.)
2. In a double boiler, melt together the chocolate and margarine. Set aside.
3. In a mixing bowl with a pouring spout, combine sugar, whole-wheat flour, egg whites, and vanilla extract. Add chocolate mixture, blending well.
4. Pour the batter into the paper-lined minimuffin tins.
5. Bake for 12 minutes or until a toothpick inserted in the center of a muffin comes out with crumbs on it. The little treats will still be moist and gooey when done.
6. Remove Fudge Kisses immediately from the muffin tins. Place them on a wire rack to cool.
7. Wrap each little kiss snugly in plastic.
8. Store the whole batch in quart-size plastic bags in the refrigerator.
9. Pack 2 Fudge Kisses in each lunchbox.

Makes 12 kid-sized servings.

Berries Be Mine

1½ cups low-fat milk
1 cup unsweetened frozen
   blueberries
3 tablespoons nonfat dry
   milk powder
1 teaspoon vanilla extract
1 teaspoon honey

---

*A milk-based drink fortified
with fruit.*

---

1. In a blender jar, combine milk, frozen blueberries, milk powder, vanilla extract, and honey.
2. Cover. Blend at low speed for 15 seconds or until smooth.
3. Pour 1 cup of milk mixture into each of 2 prechilled thermos bottles.
4. Store in the refrigerator until it's time for school.

Makes 2 kid-sized servings.

SPRING

Menu

Turkey and Carrot Salad

Muffin Melbas

Oat Bran Beauties

Fruit Smoothie

Turkey and Carrot Salad

2 cups cooked and diced
  turkey breast
2 carrots, scraped and cut
  into julienne strips
1 tablespoon raisins
¼ cup low-fat lemon yogurt

*The main attraction, with a
naturally sweet cast of flavors.*

1. In a mixing bowl, combine turkey, carrot strips, raisins, and yogurt.
2. Place ⅔ cup of the turkey mixture into each of 4 small plastic containers with snap-on lids.
3. Store in the refrigerator until time to travel.
4. At lunchtime, spread the Turkey and Carrot Salad on Muffin Melbas.
5. **Be sure to add a love note:** Call our lunchbox office about return engagements.

Makes 4 kid-sized servings.

Muffin Melbas

4 plain English muffins, cut into ⅛-inch slices

Crunchy bread snacks for continuous lunchbox showings.

---

1. Preheat oven to 225 degrees.
2. Cover 2 baking sheets (15 × 10 × ½ inch) with aluminum foil. Set aside.
3. Arrange muffins on baking sheets. Bake about 1 hour or until crisp.
4. Store the munchy muffins in quart-size plastic bags in the kitchen pantry.
5. To pack for lunches, wrap 4 muffin slices snugly in plastic for each lunchbox.
6. Serve with Turkey and Carrot Salad.

Makes 4 kid-sized servings.

Oat Bran Beauties

1 cup brown sugar
½ cup margarine
1 egg white
1 cup whole-wheat flour
1 cup oat bran cereal
1 teaspoon baking soda
½ teaspoon salt
½ teaspoon cinnamon
½ cup vanilla baking chips

Oat bran fiber in a premier cookie.

1. In a mixing bowl, blend together the brown sugar, margarine, and egg white until fluffy.
2. In another bowl, mix together the whole-wheat flour, oat bran cereal, baking soda, salt, and cinnamon.
3. Combine the dry ingredients with the margarine mixture. Add the vanilla baking chips.
4. Chill dough in the refrigerator until firm.
5. Preheat the oven to 350 degrees.
6. Drop chilled dough by the tablespoon on a baking sheet covered with aluminum foil. A small ice cream scoop works great for big, thick Beauties.
7. Bake 12 minutes or until cookie tops are lightly browned.
8. Remove cookies from the baking sheet with a metal spatula. Cool to room temperature on wire racks.
9. Store the Beauties in quart-size plastic bags in the kitchen pantry.

Makes 14 kid-sized servings.

Fruit Smoothie

1 cup apricot nectar
1 cup undiluted evaporated
   skimmed milk

---

*A light lunch drink just right
for the matinee crowd.*

---

1. In a plastic pitcher, mix together the apricot nectar and evaporated milk.
2. Pour 1 cup of the juice mixture into each of 2 prechilled thermos bottles.
3. Store in the refrigerator until it's time for school.

Makes 2 kid-sized servings.

Menu

Batter Up Chicken

Sell-Out Dipping Sauce

Grand Slam Brownies

Pinch Hitter Punch

Batter Up Chicken

½ pound raw chicken breast tenderloins (16 strips)
⅓ cup seasoned bread crumbs
2 tablespoons olive oil

No need to worry about striking out with these chicken strips.

---

1. Preheat oven to 350 degrees.
2. Add chicken strips to bread crumbs, coating well. Set aside.
3. Heat olive oil in heavy skillet. Sauté coated chicken strips about 1 minute on each side or until lightly browned. Remove and drain on paper towels.
4. Place the drained chicken strips on a baking sheet covered with aluminum foil. Bake for 10 minutes. Remove from the oven.
5. Divide the baked chicken into 4 servings, with 4 strips of chicken in each serving. Wrap each serving snugly in plastic.
6. Store in the refrigerator until time to travel. Pack 1 serving of Batter Up Chicken in each lunchbox.
7. Serve with Sell-Out Dipping Sauce.

Makes 4 kid-sized servings.

Sell-Out Dipping Sauce

1 cup prepared spaghetti
sauce
½ cup frozen chopped
broccoli, thawed and
drained
½ cup grated carrots

---

*A spicy sauce that
steps up to the plate
with Batter Up Chicken.*

---

1. In a blender jar, com-
bine spaghetti sauce,
chopped broccoli, and grated carrots.
2. Cover. Blend at medium
speed for 1 minute or until
smooth.
3. Place ¼ cup of the
spaghetti sauce mixture into
each of 4 small plastic containers with snap-on lids.
4. Store in the refrigerator
until the car pool is ready
to roll.

Makes 4 kid-sized servings.

Grand Slam
Brownies

Nonstick vegetable spray
2 egg whites
¾ cup brown sugar
¼ cup vegetable oil
¼ cup low-fat milk
1 teaspoon vanilla extract
6 tablespoons cocoa
⅔ cup unsifted all-purpose
  flour
½ teaspoon baking powder
¼ teaspoon salt

*Bases are loaded with the
calcium of milk in this
chewy dessert.*

1. Prepare a square baking pan (8 × 8 × 2 inches) with nonstick vegetable spray. Set aside.
2. Preheat the oven to 350 degrees.
3. In a mixing bowl, stir together the egg whites, brown sugar, vegetable oil, low-fat milk, and vanilla extract.
4. In another bowl, mix together the cocoa, flour, baking powder, and salt.
5. Combine the dry ingredients with the brown sugar mixture.
6. Pour the batter into the prepared baking pan. Smooth the top with a spatula.

7. Bake 15 to 20 minutes or until a toothpick inserted in the center of the brownies comes out with a few crumbs on it. Do not overbake.
8. Remove from oven. Turn out of the pan immediately. Invert and cool to room temperature on a wire rack.
9. Wrap brownies snugly in plastic and store in the kitchen pantry.
10. To pack for lunchboxes, slice into squares and wrap each piece individually.

Makes 16 kid-sized servings.

Pinch Hitter Punch

1 eight-ounce container low-fat vanilla yogurt
1 cup unsweetened apple juice
5 tablespoons nonfat dry milk powder
⅛ teaspoon cinnamon

A yogurt-based drink for home-team fans.

1. In a blender jar, combine yogurt, apple juice, milk powder, and cinnamon.
2. Cover. Blend at low speed for 10 seconds or until smooth.
3. Pour 1 cup of yogurt mixture into each of 2 prechilled thermos bottles.
4. Store in the refrigerator until it's time for school.

Makes 2 kid-sized servings.

Menu

Apple Stacks

Super Scoop Veggies

Muncher Muffins

Ginger-Lime Yogurt

Apple Stacks

4 Red Delicious apples,
cored
⅓ cup orange juice
4 two-ounce slices of 97
percent lean ham

---

*This main course is
stacked with ham and a
daily dose of apple.*

---

1. Cut through each apple
twice horizontally, creating
3 equal parts.
2. Brush a small amount of
orange juice on each apple
slice, to keep the slices from
turning brown. Place the
prepared apple slices on a
paper towel.
3. Next, use a cookie cutter
to cut 2 large circles out of
each slice of ham.
4. Now reassemble each apple, alternating the 2 ham
circles between the 3 apple
slices.
5. Wrap each Apple Stack
snugly in plastic.
6. Store in the refrigerator
until time to travel.

Makes 4 kid-sized servings.

Super Scoop Veggies

¼ cup olive oil
2 tablespoons vinegar
Juice of ½ fresh lime
½ teaspoon dry mustard
1 teaspoon salt-free herb
  seasoning
2 teaspoons sugar
2 cups cooked elbow
  macaroni
1 cup sliced yellow squash
1 cup broccoli florets

Happy vegetable crunching.

1. In a jar with a tight-fitting lid, combine olive oil, vinegar, lime juice, dry mustard, herb seasoning, and sugar. Shake and set aside.
2. In a large mixing bowl, mix together cooked macaroni, yellow squash, and broccoli.
3. Add the oil and vinegar mixture, blending well.
4. Place 1 cup of prepared vegetable salad in each of 4 small plastic serving containers with snap-on lids.
5. Store in the refrigerator until the car pool is ready to roll. Don't forget to pack a fork.

Makes 4 kid-sized servings.

Muncher Muffins

1 cup whole-wheat flour
1 cup oat bran cereal
1 tablespoon baking powder
½ cup honey
1 cup low-fat milk
2 egg whites
2 tablespoons vegetable oil

---

*Oats and honey fill out these
make-ahead muffins.*

---

1. Preheat the oven to 425 degrees. Line 12 regular-size muffin tins with paper baking cups.
2. In a large mixing bowl, combine the whole-wheat flour, oat bran, and baking powder.
3. In another bowl, mix together honey, low-fat milk, egg whites, and vegetable oil. Add this mixture to the dry ingredients, stirring until blended.
4. Bake for 15 minutes or until a toothpick inserted in the center of a muffin comes out clean.
5. Remove muffins immediately from the pan. Place them on a wire rack to cool.
6. Wrap each muffin snugly in plastic.
7. Store the whole batch in a gallon-size plastic bag in the refrigerator.

Makes 12 kid-sized servings.

Ginger-Lime Yogurt

2 eight-ounce containers
  plain low-fat yogurt
1 tablespoon undiluted
  frozen limeade concen-
  trate, thawed
⅛ teaspoon ground ginger

---

*Mix and match
your favorite flavors.*

---

1. In a small mixing bowl,
combine yogurt, limeade
concentrate, and ginger,
mixing well.
2. Spoon 1 cup of the yo-
gurt mixture into each of 2
chilled plastic containers
with snap-on lids.
3. Store in the refrigerator
until time for school.

Cook's note: You'll need a
spoon to catch the yummy
flavor of this finale.

Makes 2 kid-sized servings.

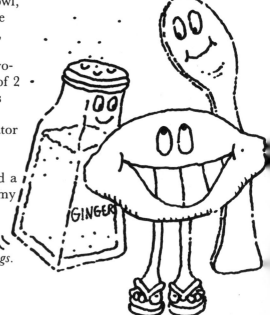

Menu

Ports Ahoy Tuna

Buccaneer Bread

Meal Maties

Set Sail Spread

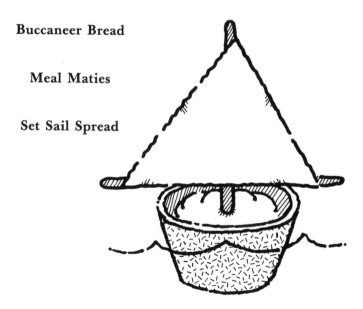

Ports Ahoy Tuna

2 cups water-packed solid
  white tuna, drained
1 cup unpeeled chopped
  apple
¼ cup chopped celery
¼ cup light mayonnaise

---

*This tuna salad is the mainstay
of a little sailor's sandwich.*

---

1. In a mixing bowl, combine tuna, chopped apple, celery, and light mayonnaise.
2. Place ¾ cup of the tuna mixture into each of 4 small plastic containers with snap-on lids.
3. Store in the refrigerator until time to set sail.
4. At lunchtime, spread the Ports Ahoy Tuna over slices of Buccaneer Bread.

Makes 4 kid-sized servings.

Buccaneer Bread

Nonstick vegetable spray
1½ cups whole-wheat flour
½ teaspoon salt
½ teaspoon baking soda
1 teaspoon cinnamon
1 cup sugar
2 egg whites
½ cup vegetable oil
1 cup frozen unsweetened
  strawberries, thawed and
  undrained

*Strawberry bread with the
bounty of whole wheat.*

1. Prepare a baking pan
(9 × 13 × 2 inches) with
nonstick vegetable spray.
Set aside.
2. Cut waxed paper to fit
the bottom of the pan.
Place carefully in the prepared pan. Set aside.
3. Preheat the oven to 350
degrees.
4. In a mixing bowl, com-
bine the whole-wheat flour,
salt, baking soda, cinna-
mon, and sugar.
5. Add the egg whites and
vegetable oil, blending well.
6. Stir in the strawberries.
7. Spoon the batter into the
prepared loaf pan.
8. Bake 50 minutes or until
a toothpick inserted in the

center of the bread comes
out clean.
9. Remove from oven.
Turn the bread out of the
pan. Cool to room temperature on a wire rack.
10. Wrap the bread snugly
in plastic and store in the
refrigerator.
11. To pack in lunchbox,
cut the bread into 12 slices
and wrap each piece in-
dividually. Pack one slice in
each lunchbox.
12. Serve with Ports Ahoy
Tuna.

Makes 12 kid-sized servings.

Meal Maties

2 large carrots, scraped,
  ends removed, and sliced
  into 16 pieces
2 large yellow squash,
  scrubbed, ends removed,
  and sliced into 16 pieces
1 green bell pepper, seeds
  removed and cut into 12
  strips

*Vegetable snacks to
munch in the galley.*

1. Place 4 carrot pieces, 4
yellow squash pieces, and 3
pepper strips into each of 4
pint-size plastic bags.
2. Drop a few ice cubes
into each bag. Close the
top. Store in the refrigerator. Drain before you pack
the snack.
3. At lunchtime, dip the
Meal Maties in Set Sail
Spread.

Makes 4 kid-sized servings.

Set Sail Spread

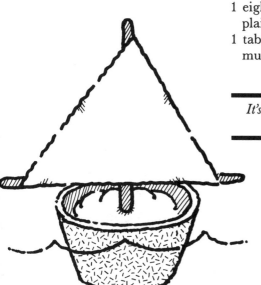

1 cup low-fat ricotta cheese
1 eight-ounce container
   plain low-fat yogurt
1 tablespoon prepared
   mustard

---

*It's anchors away with this
tangy cheese dip.*

---

1. In a small mixing bowl, blend together the cheese, yogurt, and mustard.
2. Place ¼ cup of the cheese mixture into each of 4 small plastic containers with snap-on lids.
3. Store in the refrigerator until time to cast off for school.
4. Serve with Meal Maties.

Makes 4 kid-sized servings.

Menu

Pizza Pies

Da Vinci Vegetables

Pisa Pineapple Skewers

That's Amore Milk

Pizza Pies

4 English muffins, split and toasted
4 tablespoons prepared spaghetti sauce
4 one-ounce slices cooked turkey breast
4 tablespoons shredded zucchini
4 teaspoons grated Parmesan cheese

The fun of pizza in a lunchbox sandwich.

1. Spread 1 tablespoon of spaghetti sauce on each of 4 toasted English muffin halves.
2. Place 1 slice of folded cooked turkey breast on each prepared muffin half.
3. Layer 1 tablespoon zucchini and 1 teaspoon Parmesan cheese over turkey slice.
4. Top with remaining muffin halves.
5. Wrap each Pizza Pie snugly in plastic.
6. Store in the refrigerator until time to travel. Pack 1 Pizza Pie in each lunchbox.

Makes 4 kid-sized servings.

Da Vinci Vegetables

1 large carrot, scraped and cut into 8 sticks
8 jumbo pitted black olives

Vegetable crunch tucked in an olive.

---

1. Push a carrot stick through the hole in each black olive.
2. Wrap each vegetable stick snugly in plastic. Secure ends with twist ties.
3. Store in the refrigerator until you pack the snack. Place 2 Da Vinci Vegetable snacks in each lunch bag.

Makes 4 kid-sized servings.

Pisa Pineapple Skewers

8 four-inch wooden
skewers*
8 one-inch cubes fresh
pineapple
8 one-inch cubes cantaloupe
melon
8 one-inch cubes honeydew
melon

---

*A zesty blend of fresh fruits
that towers above the
taste of canned fruit.*

---

1. Push each wooden skewer through a cube of pineapple, a cube of cantaloupe, and a cube of honeydew melon.
2. Wrap each skewer snugly in plastic. Secure ends with twist ties.
3. Store in the refrigerator until the car pool is ready to roll. Pack 2 Pisa Pineapple Skewers in each lunchbox.

Makes 4 kid-sized servings.

* Recommended for use by children over 5 years of age with adult supervision

That's Amore Milk

Great grape taste in a shake.

1 eight-ounce container low-fat blueberry yogurt
½ cup unsweetened grape juice
½ cup undiluted evaporated skimmed milk

1. In a blender jar, combine yogurt, grape juice, and evaporated milk.
2. Cover. Blend at low speed for 10 seconds or until smooth.
3. Pour 1 cup of yogurt mixture into each of 2 prechilled thermos bottles.
4. Store in the refrigerator until it's time for school.

Makes 2 kid-sized servings.

Menu

Chick-Pea Salad

Crispy Jicama Critters

Peachy Shortcakes

Milk Malted

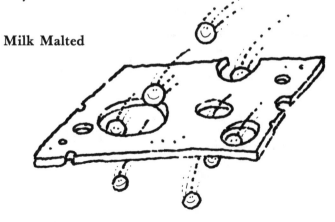

Chick-Pea Salad

2 cups diced cooked chicken
½ cup frozen English peas, thawed
½ cup shredded low-fat Swiss cheese
2 tablespoons minced red bell pepper
¼ cup plain low-fat yogurt

A main course packed with protein.

1. In a medium bowl, combine the chicken, English peas, Swiss cheese, pepper, and yogurt.
2. Place 3/4 cup of the chicken mixture into each of 4 small plastic containers with snap-on lids.
3. Store in the refrigerator until time to travel.
4. At lunchtime, spread the Chick-Pea Salad on Crispy Jicama Critters.

Makes 4 kid-sized servings.

Crispy Jicama Critters

⅓ cup fresh lime juice
1 large jicama, peeled and
   cut into 16 slices about ¼
   inch thick

---

*Jicama offers a sweet crunch
that brings kids back for more.*

---

1. In a medium mixing bowl, combine the lime juice with 1 cup of tap water. Set aside.
2. Place all of the jicama slices in the lime water, adding more water to cover if necessary.
3. Let the jicama slices soak for a few minutes.
4. Drain the jicama, discarding the lime water.
5. Using large metal cookie cutters, cut the desired animal shapes from the jicama slices.
6. Wrap each Jicama Critter snugly in plastic. Secure the ends with twist ties.
7. Store in the refrigerator until the car pool is ready to roll.
8. Pack 2 Jicama Critters in each lunchbox. Serve with Chick-Pea Salad.

Makes 4 kid-sized servings.

Peachy Shortcakes

2 cups multigrain breakfast cereal
1 cup low-fat milk
½ cup sugar
½ cup vegetable oil
¼ cup honey
3 egg whites
1 teaspoon vanilla extract
1 cup all-purpose flour
1 teaspoon baking soda
⅛ teaspoon salt
½ cup diced fresh peaches

These little peach prizes perk up noontime appetites.

---

1. Preheat the oven to 400 degrees. Line 12 regular-size muffin tins with paper baking cups.
2. In a mixing bowl, combine all ingredients except peaches.
3. Using an electric mixer, blend at medium speed for 6 minutes.
4. Spoon the batter into the paper-lined muffin tins. Top each muffin with diced peaches.
5. Bake for 15 minutes or until a toothpick inserted in the center of a muffin comes out clean.
6. Remove muffins immediately from the pan. Place them on a wire rack to cool.
7. Wrap each muffin snugly in plastic.
8. Store the whole batch in a gallon-size plastic bag in the refrigerator.

Makes 12 kid-sized servings.

Milk Malted

2 cups low-fat milk
¼ cup instant malted milk powder
½ teaspoon vanilla extract

A make-in-a-minute malt that's ready when the kids are.

---

1. In a blender jar, combine low-fat milk, malted milk powder, and vanilla extract.
2. Cover. Blend at low speed for 10 seconds or until smooth.
3. Pour 1 cup of the milk mixture into each of 2 prechilled thermos bottles.
4. Store in the refrigerator until it's time for school.

Makes 2 kid-sized servings.

Menu

Profitable Poultry

Fortune 500 Sauce

14-Carrot Cakes

Millionaire Milk

Profitable Poultry

2 cups cooked and diced
  turkey breast
1 pint strawberries, hulled
  and halved lengthwise
¼ honeydew melon, chilled
  and cut into bite-size
  pieces

---

*Turkey and fruit combine in a
creative main dish.*

---

1. In a medium mixing
bowl, combine turkey,
strawberries, and honeydew
melon, tossing gently to
blend.
2. Place 3/4 cup of the turkey mixture into each of 4
plastic containers with snap-
on lids.
3. Store in the refrigerator
until the market is right.
4. At lunchtime, place a
generous helping of Profitable Poultry in the center of
a 14-Carrot Cake; add Fortune 500 Sauce and fold
over.

Makes 4 kid-sized servings.

Fortune 500 Sauce

1 cup unsweetened pineapple juice
⅓ cup apricot nectar
1 tablespoon cornstarch

A naturally sweet sauce for turkey salad.

---

1. Place the pineapple juice in a small saucepan. Cook over low heat for a few minutes until the juice is hot but not boiling.

2. In a small bowl, mix together the apricot nectar and cornstarch. Pour this mixture into the heated pineapple juice.

3. Cook and stir over low heat until the sauce thickens.

4. Transfer to the refrigerator.

5. When the sauce has cooled to room temperature, remove pan from refrigerator. Place ⅓ cup Fortune 500 Sauce into each of 4 plastic containers with snap-on lids.

6. Return the individual containers of the fruit sauce to the refrigerator until you pack the snack.

7. Serve with Profitable Poultry.

Cook's note: This sauce makes a terrific topper for the Profitable Poultry salad. Strictly blue chip.

Makes 4 kid-sized servings.

14-Carrot Cakes

1 ½ cups whole-wheat flour
1 tablespoon sugar
1 teaspoon salt
1 ½ teaspoons baking powder
1 teaspoon baking soda
2 egg whites
2 cups low-fat buttermilk
2 tablespoons vegetable oil
1 cup grated carrots

Pancakes filled with the extra nutrition of beta-carotene.

---

1. In a medium mixing bowl, combine whole-wheat flour, sugar, salt, baking powder, and baking soda, blending well.
2. In another bowl, mix together egg whites and buttermilk.
3. Add the buttermilk mixture to the dry ingredients, stirring only until the dry ingredients are moistened.
4. Stir in the vegetable oil and carrots, mixing well but with as few strokes as possible.
5. Cook on a hot griddle, turning once to brown each side.
6. Place 2 cakes on a 6-inch paper plate. Wrap snugly in plastic.
7. Store in the refrigerator until the car pool is ready to roll.
8. Serve with Profitable Poultry and Fortune 500 Sauce.

Cook's note: Batter is lumpy. Two heaping tablespoons of batter will make a 5-inch carrot cake.

Makes 12 kid-sized servings.

Millionaire Milk

2 cups low-fat milk
¼ cup nonfat dry milk
  powder
2 tablespoons instant cocoa
  mix

---

*Improve your market share with
this cold dairy drink.*

---

1. In a blender jar, combine low-fat milk, milk powder, and cocoa mix.
2. Cover. Blend at low speed for 10 seconds or until smooth.
3. Pour 1 cup of milk mixture into each of 2 prechilled thermos bottles.
4. Store in the refrigerator until it's time for school.

Makes 2 kid-sized servings.

Menu

Chunky Cheese

Bagel Bites

Garden Grazer

Citrus Shake

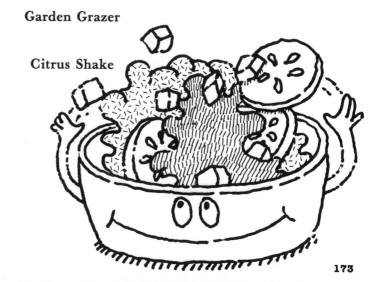

Chunky Cheese

1 cup low-fat cottage cheese
1 cup shredded 97 percent
  lean ham
⅓ cup sliced celery
⅓ cup grated carrots
Dash of garlic powder

---

*A delightfully different
bread spread.*

---

1. In a small bowl, combine cottage cheese, lean ham, celery, carrots, and garlic powder.
2. Place ½ cup of the cottage cheese mixture into each of 4 small plastic containers with snap-on lids.
3. Store in the refrigerator until time to travel.
4. At lunchtime, spoon the cheese spread onto Bagel Bites.

Makes 4 kid-sized servings.

Bagel Bites

4 plain bagels

---

*Enjoy these thin, crispy bites as
snacks or as chips with a dip.*

---

1. Cut each bagel into 6 thin slices, about ¼-inch thick.
2. Preheat the oven to 225 degrees. Cover 2 baking sheets (15 × 10 × ½ inch) with aluminum foil.
3. Arrange bagel slices on the baking sheets. Bake about 1 hour or until crisp.
4. Store Bagel Bites in quart-size plastic bags in the kitchen pantry.
5. To pack for lunch, wrap 6 Bagel Bites snugly in plastic for each lunchbox.
6. Serve with Chunky Cheese.

Makes 4 kid-sized servings.

Garden Grazer

2 cups mixed lettuce greens, including spinach
½ cup finely chopped cucumber
½ cup diced tomato

Garden vegetables rich in vitamins A and C.

---

1. In a small bowl, combine lettuce mixture, cucumber, and diced tomato, tossing gently to blend.
2. Place ½ cup of the salad into each of 4 small plastic containers with snap-on lids.
3. Store in the refrigerator until the car pool is ready to roll.

Makes 4 kid-sized servings.

Citrus Shake

2 cups low-fat milk
1 tablespoon undiluted
  frozen orange juice concentrate, thawed

---

*Orange juice and milk
team up in a
thirst-quenching beverage.*

---

1. In a plastic pitcher, mix together the milk and juice concentrate.
2. Pour 1 cup of the milk mixture into each of 2 prechilled thermos bottles.
3. Store in the refrigerator until it's time for school.

Makes 2 kid-sized servings.

Menu

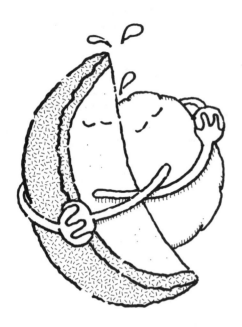

Barbecue Chicken

Cabbage Slaw

Cornmeal Muffins

Fruit Squeeze

Barbecue Chicken

1 tablespoon orange juice
2 teaspoons Worcestershire
sauce
4 tablespoons ketchup
1 teaspoon honey
1 teaspoon molasses
2 cups cooked and diced
chicken

*A protein salad with the flavor
of barbecue.*

1. In a small mixing bowl,
combine the orange juice,
Worcestershire sauce, ketchup, honey, and molasses.
2. Add the chicken to the
ketchup mixture, blending
well.
3. Place ½ cup of the prepared chicken into each of 4
plastic serving containers
with snap-on lids.
4. Store in the refrigerator
until time to travel.

Makes 4 kid-sized servings.

Cabbage Slaw

2 tablespoons undiluted frozen apple juice concentrate, thawed
2 tablespoons light mayonnaise
1 cup shredded cabbage
1 cup grated carrots
1 tablespoon raisins

Crunchy — just the way cowboys like it.

1. In a small bowl, combine apple juice concentrate with light mayonnaise. Set aside.
2. In another bowl, mix together the cabbage, carrots, and raisins, tossing to blend.
3. Add the salad dressing to the cabbage mixture, stirring well.
4. Place ½ cup of the slaw into each of 4 plastic containers with snap-on lids.
5. Store in the refrigerator until it's time to pack up the saddlebags.

Makes 4 kid-sized servings.

Cornmeal Muffins

¾ cup all-purpose flour
2½ teaspoons baking
  powder
¾ teaspoon salt
½ cup yellow cornmeal
2 egg whites
¾ cup low-fat milk
1 tablespoon honey
2 tablespoons vegetable oil

*This fancy cornbread is
downright delicious.*

1. Preheat the oven to 400 degrees. Line 12 regular-size muffin tins with paper baking cups.
2. In a small mixing bowl, combine flour, baking powder, and salt. Stir in the cornmeal.
3. Make a well in the center of the dry ingredients. Add the egg whites, milk, honey, and vegetable oil.
4. Spoon the batter into the paper-lined muffin tins. Bake for 15 to 20 minutes or until a toothpick inserted in the center of a muffin comes out clean.
5. Remove muffins immediately from the pan. Place them on a wire rack to cool.
6. Wrap each muffin in plastic.
7. Store the whole batch in a gallon-size plastic bag in the refrigerator.

Makes 12 kid-sized servings.

Fruit Squeeze

½ cup orange juice
⅓ small cantaloupe, seeds
   and rind discarded and
   the flesh cut into pieces
1 cup undiluted evaporated
   skimmed milk

A highfalutin fruit drink.

1. In a blender jar, combine the orange juice, pieces of cantaloupe, and evaporated milk.
2. Cover. Blend at low speed for 15 seconds or until smooth.
3. Pour 1 cup of cantaloupe mixture into each of 2 prechilled thermos bottles.
4. Store in the refrigerator until the car pool is ready to ride.

Makes 2 kid-sized servings.

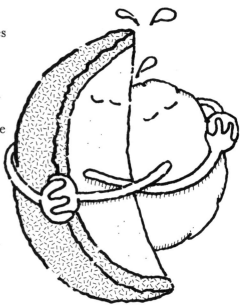

Menu

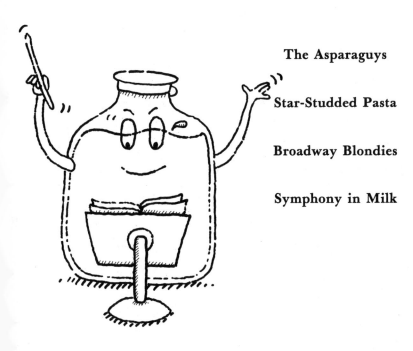

The Asparaguys

Star-Studded Pasta

Broadway Blondies

Symphony in Milk

The Asparaguys

Asparaguys:
8 cherry tomatoes
8 one-ounce slices 97 percent lean ham
8 slender stalks of fresh
asparagus, trimmed and
blanched

Held-over sauce:
1 eight-ounce container of
low-fat lemon yogurt
1 teaspoon prepared
mustard
1 teaspoon honey

---

*A meat and vegetable
main attraction.*

To assemble Asparaguys:
1. Using the pointed end of
a carrot peeler, pierce each
cherry tomato through the
stem end. Hollow out each
tomato. Set aside.
2. Roll a slice of ham
around each asparagus
stalk.
3. Push a ham-wrapped
asparagus stalk through the
hole in each cherry tomato.
4. Wrap each Asparaguy
snugly in plastic. Secure the
ends with twist ties.
5. Store in the refrigerator
until time to travel. Pack 2
Asparaguys in each
lunchbox.

To prepare sauce:
1. In a small mixing bowl,
combine yogurt, mustard,
and honey, blending well.
2. Spoon ¼ cup of the yo-
gurt mixture into each of 4
small plastic containers with
snap-on lids.
3. Store in the refrigerator
until you pack the snack.

Makes 4 kid-sized servings.

Star-Studded Pasta

2 cups cooked corkscrew
   macaroni
1 small papaya, peeled,
   halved lengthwise, seeds
   removed, and cut into
   1-inch pieces
1 pint of strawberries,
   hulled and halved
   lengthwise
¼ cup prepared poppyseed
   dressing

1. In a medium mixing
bowl, combine the macaro-
ni, papaya, strawberries,
and poppyseed dressing,
tossing gently.
2. Place 1 cup of the
macaroni mixture into each
of 4 plastic containers with
snap-on lids.
3. Refrigerate until the
show gets on the road.

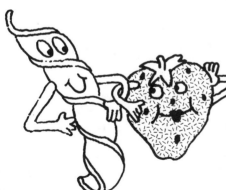

A showy pasta side dish.

Makes 4 kid-sized servings.

Broadway Blondies

1 cup margarine
1¼ cup sugar
2 egg whites
1 teaspoon vanilla extract
2 cups all-purpose flour
1 cup whole-wheat flour
1½ teaspoons cinnamon
1½ teaspoons cream of
    tartar
1 teaspoon baking soda
Pinch of salt

*Simple sugar cookies make
the last curtain call.*

1. In a mixing bowl, cream the margarine, 1 cup sugar, egg whites, and vanilla extract until fluffy.
2. In another bowl, mix together the all-purpose flour, whole-wheat flour, 1 teaspoon cinnamon, cream of tartar, baking soda, and salt.
3. Combine the dry ingredients with the margarine mixture.
4. Chill the dough in the refrigerator until firm.
5. Preheat the oven to 350 degrees.
6. In a small bowl, combine the remaining ¼ cup sugar and ½ teaspoon of cinnamon.

7. Shape the chilled dough into 1½-inch balls. Roll in sugar-cinnamon mixture.
8. Place balls 2 inches apart on baking sheets covered with aluminum foil. Flatten each ball slightly with the bottom of a measuring cup or drinking glass.
9. Bake for 10 minutes. Do not overbake or the cookies will not be soft.
10. Remove cookies from the baking sheets with a metal spatula. Cool to room temperature on wire racks.
11. Store cookies in quart-size plastic bags in the kitchen pantry.

Makes 32 kid-sized servings.

Symphony in Milk

2 cups low-fat milk
2 teaspoons undiluted
   frozen apple juice concentrate, thawed

The flavor of fruit in a milkshake.

1. In a plastic pitcher, mix together the milk and juice concentrate.
2. Pour 1 cup of the milk mixture into each of 2 prechilled thermos bottles.
3. Store in the refrigerator until it's time for school.

Makes 2 kid-sized servings.

BONUS POINTS

*How to pack surprises that nourish the ego and
add the touch of love*

Some ingredients to your child's success in life can be found in the love and security of your relationship. The note of encouragement you place next to the sandwich will go a long way toward nurturing a natural motivation to learn. The giggle your child gets from the riddle scribbled on a napkin will make him feel good inside. And the comfort he experiences in knowing that you care will inspire the self-confidence he needs to face the future.

I know that most of us have few moments to spare, so the suggestions on the following pages are as fast and easy as they are fun. Here is a sampling of simple pleasures that really score with kids:

- Pack in a photo finish. Glue an old photograph to a piece of cardboard. Cut it into jigsaw-puzzle shapes. Place it in a plastic bag with a note: "Can you figure out this photo in a flash?"

- No couture chow-bag is complete without a designer hand towel. Pick up some inexpensive washcloths at tag sales. Jazz them up with rickrack, lace, buttons — the sky's the limit. They also provide an educational exercise when smaller children get to name the colors, sort the shapes, and count the buttons.

- Turn that lunchtime treat into jolly good eating with a treasure hunt. All you need is three or four pieces of paper to write down the clues. Bury the treasure inside an empty thermos.

- Instead of lining the inside of the lunchbox with a paper towel, wrap up those favorite flavors with colored tissue paper. This brightens up special occasions and costs only a fraction of a penny per box.

- Personalize what you pack with name cards or gift tags written in secret code. (Only your child knows for sure.) For a more artistic endeavor, use nontoxic paint pens or markers to decorate plain labels.

- Dress up dried fruit in midget paper or foil baking cups. They make nifty little bowls for nuts and seeds, too.

- Who says greeting cards are just for birthdays? Pick up a few extras whenever it's handy. You'll tuck in a special sentiment that sends salutations all the way to school.

- For Christmas cheer on the day of the class party, send lunches along in a holiday stocking. There will be lots of ho-ho-hoing in the lunchroom with this festive touch.

- Add a winning recipe on a 3 × 5 notecard. Let's see: "Mix 1 part ability with 3 parts desire. Stir in some enthusiasm. Season with commitment. Makes 1 big batch of success."

- One of the prerequisites for graduating to the first grade is knowing how to tie your shoes. Practice makes perfect. Lace up a tiny box top with a not-too-sweet treat like raisins snuggled inside for your aspiring first grader.

- Perk up containers for cereal snacks, salads, and vegetable sticks by using paper drinking cups. Simply cover with plastic wrap and seal with a rubberband around the top.

- A special muffin wrapped in brightly colored cellophane helps to boost brainpower for the spelling bee.

- 'Tis the season to be jingling when bells are tied to the handle of a cardboard gift box for a holiday lunch feast.

- Kids love guessing games. Here's a new one: List interesting hints about one of your youngster's heroes on a card. (Be sure to include yourself on the hero list.) Put the card in the lunchbox. Write the answer on a piece of masking tape and put it inside the game player's coat pocket.

- Turn paper sacks into pets. Cut out a construction-paper face for a dog, cat, bear, or bunny. Decorate plastic or paper drinking cups, too.

- Encourage your children to use their noodle with picture power. Try your hand at doodling picture clues on a piece of paper, or cut out photos from magazines. Wrap the answers to the picture puzzle around a new pencil or pen.

- Surprise your child with a new friend for lunch. Draw a happy face on a small paper plate and tape it to the inside of the lunchbox lid.

- Place all of the ingredients for a sandwich in separate containers in the lunchbox. Enclose a blueprint on how to build a skyscraper sandwich. This provides good practice in following directions.

- Valentine's Day won't ever be the same after you launch Cupid's campaign from this lunchbox. Here's how:

  Cut two large red hearts out of felt fabric. Stitch the sides together, creating a heart-shaped pouch. Sew a button or a few snaps along the top so it will open and close easily. Decorate the outside with fabric trim and ribbon. Use fabric glue to move this project along quickly. Fill it up with lunch-pouch treats. After lunch, use it to pack away all of the special valentines received.

- Sticker your way to stardom by decorating plastic-wrapped food items and napkins with a few of your children's favorite stick-ons. Add to the fun by drawing in dialogue, creating an adventure story, or writing a poem to go with each sticker.

- On rainy days, pack a picnic with a checkered cloth napkin, favorite foods, and something to drink. Draw in a few ants on the paper plate to make the outdoor scene complete.

- Carry those goodies down the bunny trail in an Easter basket covered with a brightly colored cloth. Include a crayon so your little artist can draw flowers on the cloth, to make the basket a garden of delights.

- Are the kids tired of looking at the same old plastic utensils in the lunchbox? Design your own flatware. Yes, you can. Decorate the handles of plastic spoons and forks with nontoxic paint. Whatever design you choose, it will be the talk of the table in the cafeteria. Be sure to limit your creativity to the handle of the utensil and not the part that goes into the child's mouth.

osity, when nourished, become key ingredients to success in life. Take time to nurture your child's ego. The gift of yourself is priceless, and the simple pleasures you provide will be tucked away in your child's lunchbox of memories for a lifetime.

These projects are small pleasures that complement the wonderful gifts your child already possesses. The childhood qualities of optimism, enthusiasm, creativity, and curi-

BIBLIOGRAPHY

American Diabetes Association and the American Dietetic Association. *Exchange Lists for Meal Planning.* Alexandria, Virginia. 1986.

American Dietetic Association. *The Dietary Guidelines: Seven Ways to Help Yourself to Good Health and Nutrition.* Chicago. 1987.

American Heart Association. *The American Heart Association Diet: An Eating Plan for Healthy Americans.* No. 51-018-B. Dallas. 1985.

Berg, Elizabeth. "Two-Minute Treasures." *Parents Magazine* Vol. 63, No. 3 (March 1988).

Brody, Jane E. *Jane Brody's Nutrition Book.* New York: W. W. Norton. 1985.

Church, H. N., and Pennington, J. A. *Bowes and Church's Food Values of Portions Commonly Used,* 14th edition. Philadelphia: J. B. Lippincott. 1985.

Committee on Dietary Allowances, Food and Nutrition Board, National Research Council. *Recommended Dietary Allowances,* 9th edition. Washington, D.C.: National Academy of Sciences. 1980.

Corbin, Cheryl. *Nutrition.* New York: Holt, Rinehart and Winston. 1980.

Hausman, Patricia. *New American Eating Guide.* Washington, D.C.: Center for Science in the Public Interest. 1979.

Lance, Sarah. "School Lunches That Pass the Nutrition Test." *Cooking Light Magazine* Vol. 1, No. 4 (September/October 1987).

Mauer, Alvin. "Dietary Cholesterol Recommendations for Children." *Contemporary Nutrition* Vol. 12, No. 5 (1987).

McWilliams, Margaret. *Nutrition for the Growing Years.* New York: John Wiley and Sons. 1975.

National Dairy Council. *Guide to Good Eating: A Recommended Daily Pattern.* Rosemont, Illinois. 1987.

Satter, Ellyn. *How to Get Your Kid to Eat . . . But Not Too Much.* Palo Alto, California: Bull Publishing. 1987.

Shils, M. E., and Young, V. R. *Modern Nutrition in Health and Disease.* Philadelphia: Lea and Febiger. 1988.

Skodack, Nancy. *Let's Get Cookin' With the Health Heroes.* Dallas: Humana. 1987.

U.S. Department of Agriculture. *Handbook of the Nutritional Contents of Foods.* New York: Dover Publications. 1975.

U.S. Department of Agriculture. *Nutrition and Your Health: Dietary Guidelines for Americans.* Home and Garden Bulletin No. 232, edition 2. Washington, D.C. 1985.

INDEX

Z